The Pug Handbook

Brenda Belmonte

BARRON'S

Dedication

This book is dedicated to the many people who made my life with Pugs possible.

To Robert and Jean Anderson, Patti Kolesar-Stoltz, and Kay Sisson I send a heartfelt thank you. Each of you has been an incredible mentor. I wouldn't have been able to write this without your influence.

To Dr. Christine Dresser, whose tireless efforts on behalf of Pug health have helped shape health screening for the betterment of the breed. To Dr. Kimberly Greer, for her work towards solving the Pug Dog Encephalitis mystery, to Dr. Amber Labelle for her efforts to help eliminate eye diseases in the Pug, and to Dr. Kathleen Smiler for her ongoing work on spinal diseases. Each of you volunteered your time and provided up-to-date information to help me give other Pug owners what they need to make good health decisions for their Pug(s).

There are so many other dedicated veterinarians who are working to help improve our breed. I would like to give each of you a personal thank you! Our breed is healthier because of your efforts!

About the Author

Brenda Belmonte's love of Pugs began over 30 years ago. Her Brenich Pugs continue to be successful in both the conformation rings and obedience. She is a Judges Education Instructor for the Pug Dog Club of America, and an approved breed mentor. Brenda has been the practice manager for a veterinary clinic for more than 25 years, specializes in behavior and nutrition, and provides guidance and behavioral services for new puppy owners.

A Note from the Author

Throughout this book, I have used the pronoun "he" when referring to a Pug and "she" when referring to the owner or trainer. This has been done to avoid the use of the impersonal "it," or having to alternate the use of "he" in one chapter and "she" in another. No gender bias is intended by this writing style.

All inquiries should be addressed to:
Barron's Educational Series, Inc.
250 Wireless Boulevard
Hauppauge, New York 11788
www.barronseduc.com

ISBN: 978-1-4380-0276-7
Library of Congress Control Number: 2013950412

Printed in China
9 8 7 6 5 4 3 2 1

Photo Credits

Seth Casteel: back cover (top), 5, 29, 30, 38, 96, 100, 109. Dreamstime: Bytmoral: 150; Daniela Jakob: 70, 136; Yuri Arcurs: 118 iStock: AGI Photoproductions: vi; Calero: 18; ChristinaKurtz: 14; cynoclub: 42; dlewis33: viii; Fredrik Persson: 126; fstop123: 107; GlobalP: 8, 31; iculizard: 125; mabe123: 32; mariakbell: 157; Quirex: 11; s-dimit: vii; SashaFoxWalters: 26; Superflylmages: 57; TerryJ: 58, 74, 102, 113, 132; TreyMo: 97; WilleeCole: 25. Daniel Johnson: 37, 46, 78, 80, 83, 99, 161. Paulette Johnson: 52, 89, 91, 131, 146. Shutterstock: Alexander Mozymov: 15; Alis Leonte: 39, 149; Antonio Diaz: 87; Aseph: 36, 114, 128; B. Stefanov: 21; BlueSkyImage: 62; Carlos Restrepo: 158; Clesimo: 22; cynoclub: spine; Dancestrokes: 138; dezi: 16; DRS PHOTOGRAPHY: 122; Elisabeth Hammerschmid: front cover (bottom); Eric Isselee: front cover (left), back cover (bottom), 50, 56, 142; Ermolaev Alexander: 45; evastudio: 165; Forewer: 23; fstockfoto: 6; Gelpi JM: front cover (top), 10, 94, 104; Gemenacom: 152; GorillaAttack: 101, 120; GVictoria: inside front cover; Ilja Generalov: 154; Jagodka: 1; Karel Tatransky: 61; Kitch Bain: 71; Heatlher LaVeille: 35; Liliya Kulianionak: 93; Mariematata: 135; Mark Herreid: 145; Mathew Benoit: 116; Mila Atkovska: 54; mlorenz: 40, 84; NatUlrich: 67; Olga Berezhna: 164; Pavel Hlystov: 63; rangtheclick: 77; s5fotke: 144; Sinseeho: 76; spilman: 53, 162; steamroller_blues: 12; Utekhina Anna: inside back cover, 4; VKarlov: 2, 167; Viorel Sima: 72, 110; WilleeCole: 64, 68, 141. Kira Stackhouse: 28.

Important Note

This pet owner's guide is designed to help readers learn how to buy or adopt and care for a Pug. The author and the publisher consider it important to point out that the advice given in this book is meant primarily for normally developed dogs of excellent physical health and good character.

Anyone who adopts a fully grown dog should be aware that the animal has already formed its basic impression of human beings. The new owner should watch the animal carefully, including its behavior toward humans.

If the Pug comes from a rescue organization or shelter, it may be possible to get some information on the dog's background and previous history. There are dogs that, as the result of bad experiences, behave in an unnatural manner or may bite. Only people that have experience with dogs should take in such animals.

Caution is further advised in the association of children with dogs, in meeting other dogs, and in exercising the dog without a leash.

Even well-behaved and carefully supervised Pugs sometimes do damage to their owner's property, to the property of others, or cause accidents. It is therefore in the owner's interest to be adequately insured against such eventualities, and we strongly urge all dog owners to purchase a liability policy that covers their dog.

Contents

Chapter One

Pugs from the Past

Far East Origins

The Pug is thought to be one of the oldest breeds on record. References to Pug-type dogs have been documented as early as 551 B.C. by Confucius, who mentioned short-mouthed dogs. The exact ancestry of the Pug is not known however, and has been the subject of much discussion and controversy. The most common theory is that today's Pug is Chinese in origin. Several breeds may have been part of what has now become the modern-day Pug, with the Chinese Lo-Sze or "Foo Dog" most closely resembling early Pugs.

Descriptions of the Lo-Sze depict a compact, flat-faced dog with a short, close-fitting coat. The skin of the Lo-Sze was said to be elastic and the forehead of most specimens contained wrinkles forming a W, closely resembling the Chinese character for Prince. This wrinkling became known as the "Prince Mark." Two ear types have been described in the Lo-Sze— one was small and often compared to a dried half of an apricot, the other a "horn ear." These two ear types are now known on today's modern Pug as the "Button" and "Rose" ears, respectively.

The tail of the Lo-Sze was commonly docked, though tails with both single and double curls have been described. The color of the Lo-Sze was varied with many black and white specimens described. A white blaze was present on the forehead in some dogs and the Lo-Sze may also have been the predecessor of today's modern Pekingese.

The Lo-Sze or early Pug was considered to have been a prize possession by the Chinese Emperors.

Many were afforded their own palace rooms, and some were even guarded by soldiers. Foo Dogs were immortalized in ancient Chinese scrolls, sculptures, and numerous paintings. The breeding records of Chinese empress Tsu-Hsi in the mid-1800s clearly show that at that time there were two distinguishable breeds in favor, the longer-legged, short-coated Lo-Sze and the shorter, long-coated Pekingese. Solid black puppies were considered to be a symbol of bad luck, and it is believed that most were destroyed at birth.

European Movement

Wherever the Pug goes, he quickly moves to the forefront of popularity. In the late sixteenth century, development of trade routes between Europe and the Far East brought

the Pug into the Netherlands, Portugal, Spain, France, and England. It is widely believed that sailors gave Pugs as gifts to their loved ones upon returning home from the Far East.

Russia's first ambassador to China was said to have received several Pugs as gifts, which created a new popularity in Russia. The Princess Provost Hedwig Sophie Augusta (the aunt of Catherine the Great) was an avid animal lover. While she is thought to have owned many breeds, her favorite was the Pug. She was known to travel with as many as 16 Pugs and one was always allowed to accompany her to church.

When the Spanish attempted to take control of Holland in the late 1500s, a Pug believed to be named "Pompey" is credited with saving the life of Prince William of Orange. It has been reported that Prince William was alerted to the midnight attack by his Pug. Prince William narrowly escaped as his camp was destroyed. Upon his return to power, Prince William proclaimed the Pug as the honored dog of the Dutch ruling house.

The Spanish Painter Francisco Goya used a fawn Pug in his portrait "The Marquesa," painted in 1786.

In France, many admired the Pug. Louis XV, King of France, often commissioned portraits of his favorite objects and activities. Jean-Baptiste Oudry painted "Pug Dog," thought to be a portrait of one of Louis XV's most treasured dogs. Portraits of King Louis XV's mistresses were also common and both Madame de Pompadour and Madame du Barry owned Pugs, presumably gifts from Louis XV. Perhaps the most infamous Pug in France was "Fortune," the beloved Pug of Napoleon's Josephine. Fortune was said to have carried messages under his collar between his mistress and Napoleon Bonaparte. It is well known that on their wedding night, Fortune's intent to keep Josephine for himself created a problem for Napoleon and he was able to join his bride only after enduring several bites to the legs from Fortune. Neither was presumed happy about the arrangement.

The Pug in England

It is in England where the blueprint for today's Pug was created. More history is documented about the Pug in England than in any other European country, demonstrating the fondness of the English for the Pug. It is in England that the name "Pug" was first used, derived from the Latin word *pugnus* meaning fist. This description is used in reference to the side profile of the Pug's head, which resembles the shape of a closed fist. The term "Pug" soon became a term of endearment in England, again illustrating a love for the breed.

When Prince William of Orange came to power as King of England

❖ PUG POINT ❖

Special Names

Each European country had a special name for the Pug. Some of its common names were
• Ha Ba Gou (Chinese)
• MopsHond (Dutch)
• Mops (Swedish)
• Mopsi (Finnish)
• MopsHund (German)
• Carlin (Old French)
• Carlino (Italian)
• Doguillo (Spanish)
• Smutmhadra (Irish Gaelic for stumpy dog)

in 1688, he brought with him a large number of Pugs. The Pug remained a favorite of British royalty and nobility, many immortalized in paintings. Other notable royalty smitten by the "Pug Bug" were Queen Victoria, Queen Mary II Stuart, and the Duke and Duchess of Windsor.

The famous English painter William Hogarth was noted for his many paintings incorporating Pugs. His own Pug "Trump" was often portrayed in his work and it is his 1730 painting "House of Cards" that depicts an early black Pug. Trump was also said to be the model for sculptor Louis-François Roubiliac, whose works in porcelain were produced by the Chelsea Pottery Company, as well as German sculptor Johann Joachim Kaendler, whose Meissen porcelain Pugs are highly collectable today.

By the mid 1800s, two distinct strains began to appear and dominate English bloodlines. The earliest is believed to have been the Morrison line. The Morrison strain is said to have descended from the bloodlines of Queen Charlotte, wife of George III. The second strain, founded on import bloodlines from Russia and perhaps Hungary, was that of Lord and Lady Willoughby d'Eresby. The Windsor Pugs belonging to Queen Victoria were said to have come from both the Morrison and Willoughby strains. It was Queen Victoria who banned ear cropping in Pugs, citing the procedure as unnecessary cruelty.

The invasion of China during the reign of Tsu-Hsi, and the looting of the Palace that followed, brought many new dogs into England. Pugs imported from China in the late 1800s more closely resembled today's Pugs, with shorter legs and a much shorter nose. The Pug Dog Club of England was established in 1883.

The Color Controversy

Early Pugs of the 1800s were documented in a variety of colors. The preferred color was golden fawn, with variations in shades ranging from light fawn or cream to a golden apricot color. It is in this color range that the Morrison Pugs are best known. Willoughby Pugs were described as a cold, fawn color with some references to a silver-gray or stone gray color. The black mask was not as common as it is today and was considered a great asset. The "Prince" mark, known today as the thumbprint, was also a prized feature. Many references exist to indicate that some strains of fawn Pugs had a fair amount of white on the legs and chest, a disqualification today.

The origin of the black Pug has never been accurately established. The most widely believed theory is that Lady Brassey of Sussex, England, imported two black Pugs from China in 1877. Queen Victoria owned several black Pugs, however, with photographs of black Pugs appearing in her albums as early as 1854. Lady Brassey did have perhaps the largest number of black Pugs in the late 1800s and her breeding program

---

❖ PUG POINT ❖

Meissen Pugs

Pugs from the Meissen collection often have cropped ears, long legs, and a fairly long muzzle. These features were common in Pugs of the eighteenth and early nineteenth centuries.

defined the look of black Pugs in England for many years.

The first black Pugs were exhibited in England at the first Pug Dog Club Show in June 1885. Lady Brassey herself exhibited one of her blacks at the Maidstone All-Breed Show in 1886. The Pugs descending from Lady Brassey's bloodlines often had a white chest and white feet. Many of Queen Victoria's own blacks in the late 1800s descended from the Brassey strain. The Mortival Strain of Pugs became the first bloodline of black Pugs in England to be virtually clear of white.

The exact origin of the silver Pug is unknown. Queen Victoria is thought to have owned two silver-gray Pugs, Ayah and Mops. References to other silver pugs are scarce, but a "blue" Pug was reported to have been born in 1913

Early American Pugs

The exact date marking the Pug's arrival in America is uncertain. Dr. M. H. Cryer is thought to be one of the earliest breeders of Pugs in the United States. Analyses of early pedigrees indicate that Dr. Cryer's imports from England were directly related to Click, whose parents were Lamb and Moss. Records indicate that 24 Pugs were exhibited in 1879 at a show in New York. The American Kennel Club accepted the Pug in 1885. True to his past history, the Pug became quite popular in the United States during the early 1900s. The Pug's popularity suffered during World War I; however, formation of the Pug Dog Club of America in 1931 signaled a new era of popularity for the Pug.

Chapter Two
Pugs in the Present

Following in the footsteps of his ancestors in other countries, the Pug remains a very popular breed in the United States. While the breed has seen some decline in popularity over the last decade, in 2012 the American Kennel Club ranked the Pug at number 30 in popularity of all breeds and the eighth most popular toy breed. Ask any Pug owner what makes the breed so endearing and you will undoubtedly get many different answers reflecting the Pug's "larger than life" attitude, jolly personality, and comical expressions. Since his arrival in the United States in the late 1800s, the Pug has had some noticeable changes.

While descriptions of the English Pugs of the early 1800s began to define correct color, the term "Victorian Pug" has been used to indicate correct type in the early Pug. The Victorian Pugs had more length of leg, a more prominent nose, and a smaller, high-set ear. It is not uncommon to hear "Victorian type" used to describe any Pug that appears taller and thinner or one that has a bit more length of nose. Victorian-type Pugs are commonly seen in old paintings and many works of art.

It was the 1900s in the United States when the overall look of today began to take shape. The description of today's Pugs can be best summarized with the following description: round head, square (compact) body, and curly tail. These features combined create the overall balance and unmistakable look of the Pug. The Pug today has more thickness in body and diameter of bone than its early counterparts, a larger head with a more prominent nose roll, less length of nose, and a flatter skull profile when viewed from the side.

American Kennel Club Breed Standard

The Pug has remained virtually unchanged since his acceptance into the American Kennel Club in 1885. Some slight revisions to the standard were made in 1991. A more significant revision was made in 2008, when a disqualification was added to prohibit Pugs from being exhibited that were not black or fawn.

General appearance: Symmetry and general appearance are decidedly square and cobby. A lean, leggy Pug and a dog with short legs and a long body are equally objectionable.

Size, proportion, substance: The Pug should be *multum in parvo*, or "a lot of dog in a little space," and this condensation (if the word may be used) is shown by compactness of form, well-knit proportions, and hardness of developed muscle. Weight from 14 to 18 pounds (dog or bitch) desirable. *Proportion:* square.

Head: The *head* is large, massive, round, not apple-headed, with no indentation of the *skull*. The *eyes* are dark in color, very large, bold and prominent, globular in shape, soft and solicitous in *expression*, very lustrous, and, when excited, full of fire. The *ears* are thin, small, soft, like black velvet. There are two kinds: the "rose" and the "button." Preference is given to the latter. The *wrinkles* are large and deep. The *muzzle* is short, blunt, square, but not upfaced. *Bite:* A Pug's bite should be very slightly undershot.

Neck, Topline, Body: The *neck* is slightly arched. It is strong, thick, and with enough length to carry the head *proudly*. The short *back* is level

from the withers to the high tailset. The *body* is short and cobby, wide in chest, and well ribbed up. The *tail* is curled as tightly as possible over the hip. The double curl is perfection.

Forequarters: The *legs* are very strong, straight, of moderate length, and are set well under. The *elbows* should be directly under the withers when viewed from the side. The *shoulders* are moderately laid back. The *pasterns* are strong, neither steep nor down. The *feet* are neither so long as the foot of the hare, nor so round as that of the cat; well split-up toes, and the nails black. Dewclaws are generally removed.

Hindquarters: The strong, powerful hindquarters have moderate bend of *stifle* and short *hocks* perpendicular to the ground. The *legs* are parallel when viewed from behind. The hindquarters are in balance with the forequarters. The *thighs* and *buttocks* are full and muscular. *Feet* as in front.

Coat: The coat is fine, smooth, soft, short, and glossy, neither hard nor woolly.

Color: The colors are fawn or black. Fawn color should be decided so as to make the contrast complete between the color and the trace and the mask.

Markings: The *markings* are clearly defined. The muzzle or mask, ears, moles on cheeks, thumb mark, or diamond on forehead, and the back trace should be as black as possible. The mask should be black. The more intense and well defined it is, the better. The trace is a black line extending from the occiput to the tail.

Gait: Viewed from the front, the forelegs should be carried well forward, showing no weakness in the pasterns, the paws landing squarely with the central toes straight ahead. The rear action should be strong and free through hocks and stifles, with no twisting or turning in or out at the joints. The hind legs should follow in line with the front. There is a slight natural convergence of the limbs both fore and aft. A slight roll of the hindquarters typifies the gait, which should be free, self-assured, and jaunty.

Temperament: This is an even-tempered breed, exhibiting stability, playfulness, great charm, dignity, and an outgoing, loving disposition.

Disqualification: Any color other than fawn or black.

Today's Variation in Type

There is a trend that seems to occur when a breed begins to soar in the popularity charts and the demand for puppies exceeds the availability. The Pug's popularity, combined with questionable breeding practices of some individuals, has made the breed vulnerable to changes in structure and type.

While the AKC breed standard calls for a Pug to be *multum in parvo*, there are a large number of Pugs whose body shape does not meet this expectation. Pugs are expected to be compact, with strong, straight legs and well-muscled hindquarters, and should appear to be square when viewed from the side. There are more Pugs produced each year by people who do not know or understand the breed standard, or who simply breed to produce pet Pugs.

❖ PUG POINT ❖

The Pug's slight decrease in popularity may be due to the new trend of owning a "designer dog" or "hybrid breed."

Designer dogs are mixed-breed dogs that are often erroneously reported to be healthier or have fewer drawbacks to ownership, such as shedding less or being easier to housetrain. The Pug has not been spared this trend.

The Puggle is perhaps the best known designer dog—a cross between a Pug and Beagle. Some other common crosses are:

Bug—Pug/Boston Terrier
Chug—Pug/Chihuahua
Frenchipug—Pug/French Bulldog
Ori-Pei—Pug/Chinese Shar Pei
Pugalier—Pug/Cavalier King Charles Spaniel
PugAPoo—Pug/Poodle

While these hybrids may become good pets, they often do not have the same fun-loving personality of the Pug. Designer dogs can also have health problems common in one or both breeds.

These Pugs have legs that are much thinner and taller, appear to be longer in body length, and lack the large, round head and blunt, short muzzle that have made the Pug so famous. This longer, leggier look creates a Pug that almost appears to be a reproduction of those Victorian Pugs seen in the English paintings of the early 1800s.

While these Pugs are indeed pure-bred, some may almost look as if they may be mixed with some other breed. When standing next to a Pug that has been bred to compete in the show ring or one that was produced with the breed standard in mind, these "Victorian-type" Pugs are quite noticeably different. This change in type often seems to be accompanied by a departure from the normal Pug personality and temperament. Some of these Pugs appear to be hyperactive, difficult to train, and even occasionally aggressive. All these traits are the complete opposite of the fun-loving, sedate companion that many have come to know and love. However, no matter what your Pug looks like, he will have the same ability to grab attention that has made the Pug so popular.

Color Today

Coat color in Pugs has long been a source of controversy, with many Pug lovers arguing in favor of one color over another. The current AKC standard allows two colors: fawn and black.

Fawn

Fawn is the most common color today, and perhaps the most widely recognized color associated with the Pug. The revision of the American Kennel Club standard in 2008, which excluded the previous colors of apricot-fawn and silver, has created a controversy of sorts today. The term fawn now covers a wide range of color shades, varying from a rich cream to apricot. Some breeders use the term "apricot-fawn" to describe any Pug with an orange-tinted or true apricot coat color. Unscrupulous breeders may claim that they have "rare apricot" or "apricot-fawn" puppies, charging hundreds of dollars more for these puppies than their fawn littermates. These colors are not rare; they are simply now all registered as "fawn" with the American Kennel Club. Black-tipped guard hairs are not uncommon in fawn Pugs with very dark ear pigment.

Perhaps the most widely recognized characteristic of the fawn Pug is

❖ PUG POINT ❖

Trace

In fawn Pugs, the trace is a darker defined line extending down the spine, from the skull to the tail. The trace has been lost in many bloodlines, as coat color has become much lighter. The ear color has faded as well, and the toenails may be clear in some of these Pugs. Other Pugs may have excess pigment. These Pugs have jet black ears and nails, and may have a "saddle mark" as the trace has widened behind the shoulders, across and down the back.

its black mask. The black markings of the mask should cover the entire muzzle; the nose roll may be black or dark brown in color. The skin area around the eyes may be the same shade as the nose wrinkle or mask, framing the eyes and drawing your attention to those fiery "windows to a Pug's soul." The head wrinkles are shaded in black, as if someone brushed a piece of charcoal against the Pug's forehead and forgot to wipe it off. The fawn Pug's ears should be the same color as the mask, the darker the shade of black, the better!

Black

Black is the only other color recognized by the American Kennel Club in the Pug. The black coat is jet black, often described as blue-black in color, with no shades of gray, fawn, or rust. Fanciers of the black Pug will tell you that they have their own special qualities, including the tendency to shed less than fawn Pugs. Black Pugs will often appear to be more serious than their fawn counterparts. Black Pugs always seem to be analyzing each situation before reacting, while fawn Pugs are inclined to be more carefree and reckless in their actions. While it is true that you do not see the same contrast in the face of black Pugs that is apparent in the fawns, the same spirit is found in their eyes, and the wheels can be seen turning in their heads by watching their facial expressions.

While any red cast is undesirable in a black Pug, repeated exposure to sunlight can damage the black coat, giving it a red or brown tint. Excessive dead hair can also give the black coat a dull appearance.

Silver

The United Kennel Club (UKC) and the Canadian Kennel Club (CKC) both recognize the additional color of silver or silver-fawn. Silver Pugs may

also be referred to as blue Pugs but are rarely seen today. The true silver coat can best be described as a faded steel color, cold, flat, and with darker shading of the characteristic ears, mask, and trace. There are only a few breeders in the United States today who have isolated this gene and are actively breeding to heighten awareness of this unique color.

Albino

Albino Pugs are extremely rare. These Pugs have very sensitive skin and lack the darker muzzle and darker ears. Albino Pugs are often plagued with health problems due to their lack of pigment.

Albino Pugs are disqualified from conformation competition by the American Kennel Club, the United Kennel Club, and the Canadian Kennel Club.

Brindle

It is worth mentioning that brindle Pugs have gained popularity and are the subject of great controversy. While there are references in England of Pug-like dogs with brindle coats, the validity of the brindle color in the United States and Canada remains questionable. Brindle is a color disqualification as well.

White Markings

White markings can occur in all colors, with the feet and chest the most common areas affected. The Canadian Kennel Club deems white less than the size of a dime on the chest acceptable. The United Kennel Club does not address white markings in their breed standard. White spots or patches are a disqualification according to the American Kennel Club breed standard.

The Clown

What sets a Pug apart from other breeds is his ever-present sense of humor. Pugs enjoy life to the fullest. Whether the activity is eating, sleeping, or running around your furniture, tail tucked in a self-propelled "Pug run," the Pug is always trying to be the center of attention. It is the Pug's mischievous look and upbeat personality that appeals to old and young alike.

Full of natural curiosity, the Pug has a knack for finding opportunities to get into trouble. Pug owners soon learn that it is impossible to stay upset with them, as they worm their way back into your lap quickly! Pugs are very anxious to learn and ever willing to please you—as long as it is done their way. The girls in particular can be rather stubborn, and must feel that whatever task you want them to accomplish was their idea in the first place. This streak of stubbornness can be overcome with patience and an equal sense of humor on your part. The center of the universe for many Pugs is food, and they are always searching for the opportunity to "steal the show."

Pugs and Their People

If you want a guard dog or a hunting companion, the Pug is not for you. If your idea of the perfect canine is an athlete or you long for a dog that "does his own thing," do not consider a Pug. If your idea of the perfect dog is one that snuggles under the covers while taking up most of the bed, follows you like a shadow and craves attention wherever he goes, the Pug is the perfect choice. Pugs live for companionship and don't consider themselves any less human than the people they own. Pug owners are universal in their love of the breed. Stop any Pug owner to ask about her Pug and be prepared for a conversation complete with baby pictures! A quick look around and you will see many multi-Pug families. Pugs are like potato chips—you can't have just one!

Once you own a Pug, the breed becomes an addiction. Proud Pug moms wear Pug jewelry, and smitten Pug Dads adorn T-shirts proclaiming their love for the breed. Owning a Pug is not just owning a dog; it becomes a very integral part of your everyday life.

Is a Pug Right for You?

The addition of a dog to any home should be a well-thought-out, informed decision. Pugs make excellent companions and therefore cannot be left to amuse themselves. Whether your lifestyle is sedate and you enjoy sitting around watching television or are more active, enjoying walking outdoors or traveling, the Pug is quite adaptable. He prefers to be treated as just another family member, and demands to be included in most activities. He will alert you to every visitor (once they

are inside), as he seeks out every opportunity to greet new people. Don't expect a watchdog—the Pug is too lazy and only wants to amuse each new person he meets.

Children

The Pug is very tolerant of children and will happily wait beneath the chair of smaller kids, looking for those discarded leftovers. Older children find the Pug particularly attractive. Pugs consider children to be siblings and will wait patiently while homework is being finished. When it is time to go out and play, the Pug responds eagerly.

Note: Care must be taken to supervise very young children around the face of the Pug as the eyes are exposed and more vulnerable to accidental injury from little fingers.

Shedding

Every breed has its flaws and the Pug is no exception. If you are looking for a nonshedding or hypoallergenic breed, do not consider a Pug. Pugs shed guard hairs daily, while losing undercoat twice each year. During the dry winter months, they produce a significant amount of dead skin, which often triggers a positive reaction for most people with allergies to dogs.

Snoring and Sneezing

The Pug's flat face causes two unique problems: snoring and sneezing. If you are a sound sleeper, you will have no trouble with the deep, repetitive sound that a Pug

emits while resting comfortably on your pillow. When relaxed, the Pug almost "purrs" with delight. When impatient or disgusted your Pug will "sneeze," showering you as if to say, "Hurry up." Many an unsuspecting guest will find that a Pug cannot easily be ignored.

Drooling

Pugs do not drool. But they do seem to enjoy spreading their water across the floor (after all, if they stay too long to drink they might miss something!).

Contact with Owners

The Pug seems to delight in contact with his owners. Many Pugs will greet their owners by yodeling in excitement, and then grab one of their fingers and gently pull them around the room. Some of these Pugs refuse to let go, conveying, "No, please don't leave me again." Once the joy of your arrival has worn off, Pugs look for an opportunity to be close to you, rubbing their face and nose wrinkle on your pants or sleeve. The debris left behind on your clothing is a distinct reminder that your Pug loves you!

Odor

Some Pug owners complain of a "doggy" odor. The Pug is actually a relatively clean breed and excessive odors are usually the result of infections or too much moisture in the ear canal or nasal folds. Flatulence is also a common complaint, according to many Pug owners.

Chapter Three

Purchasing Your Pug Puppy

With careful consideration, you have decided that a Pug is the perfect fit for your family. Your next step is to locate a puppy and make it your own. Finding a reputable source to purchase your puppy can be a time-consuming, sometimes frustrating experience. Finding the right puppy with the temperament that best complements your lifestyle is the most important factor in creating a long-lasting bond. This new addition will be with you for some time, and making an informed decision on where and when to bring your puppy home will ensure that you and your Pug are a match made in heaven.

Pug Breeders— Who Are They?

Unfortunately, the word "breeder" has many connotations, both good and bad. There are no universal regulations or rules governing those who breed dogs. There are no schools to learn how to raise puppies correctly. It is up to you, the puppy buyer, to do your homework.

Let common sense be your guide when you are making the final purchase decision.

Show Breeders

There are four common, yet very different types of Pug breeders. The first is the "show" or "professional" breeder. Show breeders generally do not advertise in order to sell their puppies, as most are spoken for in advance through word of mouth from previous puppy buyers. Breeders who show Pugs usually belong to one or more kennel clubs, are bound by a strict code of ethics when planning to breed, and research pedigrees of perspective dogs before selecting a mate. It is not unusual for show breeders to fly across the country in order to breed to the dog they feel best suits their particular Pug's needs. Show breeders screen breeding stock for genetic problems and select only the healthiest dogs to be used for breeding.

Pets from those involved in showing are generally sold on limited registration and with a purchase contract designating a certain age

Life Expectancy

The Pug's life expectancy is generally 12 to 14 years, with individuals living as long as 16 to 17 years of age.

by which the Pug must be spayed/neutered. Do not be offended if the breeder asks dozens of questions about you and your family, your previous pets, your home life, and your interest in Pugs. These breeders are extremely picky about letting their babies go and you may feel as if you are being interrogated before you get the okay to purchase a puppy. It is not unusual for show breeders to wait until the puppies are 12 to 16 weeks old before picking your Pug for you. These breeders produce puppies only to improve the breed and therefore keep the best representations of the breed to show.

Pet Breeders

Breeders who do not show are considered by many to be "pet" or "hobby" breeders. Pet breeders often own both the sire and dam and breed to produce pet-quality puppies. These breeders often advertise in the local paper or on the Internet to sell their puppies. Pugs purchased from pet breeders are often a bit larger or taller than those from show breeders. These Pugs often have a smaller head, longer muzzle, and less substance and bone. They may also be somewhat more active than their show-bound counterparts. Pet breeders love their Pugs and want to see others enjoy the breed as well.

Commercial Breeders

Commercial breeders are large-scale breeding operations. While few commercial breeders attempt to create a positive, healthy environment for the puppies they produce, many are kept in substandard living conditions, and are unhealthy. There may be little, if any, medical care for the adult dogs and puppies.

Commercial breeders typically cannot provide accurate health information regarding the parents of the puppies they offer for sale. Few, if any, health checks are performed on breeding stock to screen for hereditary problems. Puppies that eat, sleep, and eliminate in the same small area often have difficulty when it comes to becoming house-trained in the future. A lack of early socialization may lead to behavioral problems ranging from hyperactivity and difficulty learning to shyness and fear biting.

Puppy Brokers

These are individuals who advertise on the Internet that claim to be relatives or friends of the breeder who typically lives out of state. In most cases these individuals are "brokers" acting as middlemen. Brokers may have litters of more than one breed in their home. Puppies purchased from these brokers are sometimes unhealthy. When purchasing a puppy from a broker, keep in mind that he or she may offer very little help or advice if you have a problem after you bring your puppy home.

From Your Breeder, with Love

When you have found a reputable breeder, what should you expect when purchasing your Pug puppy? First and most importantly, you expect a healthy puppy. Your puppy will be a family member and illnesses can occur. Careful breeding is the key to minimizing the diseases that can be prevented. Ask the breeder for references of previous puppy buyers and make sure to contact those people listed. These individuals are your best resource in determining whether you may encounter any long-term health problems and if the breeder has been helpful with solving problems and answering questions.

The Guarantee

Reputable breeders offer a guarantee with each puppy they produce. Pet stores and brokers may also offer a guarantee. How can you be sure that the guarantee you are being offered is going to benefit you and your puppy? Give yourself time to read the guarantee by asking for a copy before you pur-

---

❖ PUG POINT ❖

Limited Registration

Limited Registration is a designation that a breeder can use to ensure that a dog is not used for breeding purposes. Pugs with limited registration cannot be shown in conformation events, but may compete in performance events such as obedience and agility.

chase your puppy. Read the information carefully and ask questions if you do not understand the terms of the contract. The guarantee should include both a short-term and long-term health clause. While no breeder can guarantee that every Pug has a perfectly healthy life, be aware that many contracts require that you return your puppy for a replacement if there is a serious health problem. Are you willing to give up a pet that has become an important member of your family? Pay careful attention to any details that you may be required to follow regarding veterinary care, diet or supplement requirements, weight control, and future address changes. In many cases, by not adhering to these requests, you will void the guarantee.

The Waiting Game

Perhaps the most difficult part of adding a Pug to your family is waiting for the right one. Show breeders often have a waiting list of several months to several years. Hobby breeders may produce puppies more often, while brokers and pet stores have Pugs available on a regular basis. When purchasing any Pug it is always "buyer beware." Inexpensive and readily available Pugs may actually cost you more in the long run in medical expenses, training costs, and endless frustration.

What Does a Sound Puppy Look Like?

Once you have the opportunity to purchase a Pug, how can you determine which one has the "right stuff" for you? Breeders often use the word "soundness" to describe puppies. What is a sound Pug puppy? Soundness is the combination of a structurally correct, healthy puppy balanced with a confident, outgoing personality. A structurally sound Pug puppy has a thick, substantial body on four solid, sturdy legs. The correct head will be large and round, with expressive eyes that look straight ahead. Combine this look with a lively, mischievous personality, one that greets everyone with eager enthusiasm, and you have a "sound" puppy.

In addition, you should have the opportunity to evaluate the mother and perhaps the father of the puppies. The look of the parents and their personalities will give you the best idea of what to expect from your new Pug. Any shyness or aggression is unusual in Pugs and should be noted. You should also note any tendency toward hyperactivity or uncontrollable behavior. If the sire and dam are well-built, stocky examples of the breed, your puppy should mature into an excellent representative of the Pug.

Primary Socialization

A sound Pug puppy has also been raised properly, with attention paid to the sensitive social developmental

periods. Primary socialization takes place between 3 and 14 weeks of age. Your puppy's first imprint period takes place with his breeder at 4 to 6 weeks of age. During this early development phase, positive exposure to a variety of new people, sights, and sounds should have taken place.

From 6 to 8 weeks of age, Pug puppies need to be housed with their littermates. This is a crucial period of development, where puppies learn "bite inhibition," or how hard they can bite during play without causing pain to their littermates. Learning to soften biting during play is critical when your puppy begins to play with his human family members. This is also the stage of development where puppies learn to recognize body language cues that they will use when interacting with

tiveness, fearfulness, or aggressive biting during this phase should be noted, and the owner should make every effort not to reward or encourage these behaviors.

Bringing Home Baby

Anyone who has children knows that the first few weeks can be a period of adjustment for everyone involved. A new puppy is no different and each day will bring new experiences. There are several sensitive periods that your new Pug puppy will encounter. It is a good idea to be aware of these "imprint periods," so that you can tailor your puppy's experiences to create a happy, stable puppy.

The First Night

The first 24 hours are the beginning of a series of adjustments for your new Pug. Episodes of crying and confusion may be common as the search for littermates and mother begins. Keep visitors to a minimum for the first few days, even though it may be hard to resist showing off your new Pug. Your puppy's appetite may be slightly decreased in response to the lack of competition for each meal. By giving your puppy soft bedding such as a towel or sheepskin, offering a plush toy as a "littermate," and providing a quiet sleeping area, your puppy will adapt quickly to its new home.

other dogs. Puppies that have been removed from their littermates before 8 weeks of age may have trouble properly interacting with other dogs as adults.

Between 8 and 12 weeks of age, sound puppies are quite social. Sound puppies can be exposed to a variety of new stimuli and, when done properly, can learn to overcome new situations without experiencing fear. Improper or incomplete socialization during this critical stage may trigger behavior problems later on. This is also the first period that imprints fear. Painful or traumatic experiences may produce a lasting impression during the eighth, ninth, and tenth weeks of life.

The onset of adolescence is at 12 to 14 weeks of age. Positive social activities at this age should be continually encouraged. Any signs of protec-

The First Week

The first week is considered the "trial and error" period. It is during this week that feeding times, potty times, and sleep schedules are first established. Consistency on a day-to-day basis is the key. Your Pug needs to learn what to expect in your household, as well as what is acceptable behavior.

With each new day, both you and your puppy will begin to follow the same schedule. A puppy's day consists of a combination of eating, sleeping, playing, and eliminating, much like a human toddler. The success of acclimating your puppy largely depends on how quickly the puppy's normal routine can be incorporated into your schedule.

Sleep deprivation of the new Pug owner is common during the first week if there are unrealistic expectations of the puppy. If your puppy is less than 12 weeks of age, be prepared to get up with him at least once each night for a potty break. Young puppies have bladder control for only four or five hours. If your family can take turns with nighttime duties during the first few weeks, lack of sleep is kept to a minimum.

During the first week, it may not be necessary to use a leash and collar on your puppy when taking him outside to eliminate. Puppies less than 12 weeks of age feel much more comfortable when they have a central figure, or "mommy figure," to look to when a new situation arises. Within the first few hours after you return home with your puppy, you

should begin to teach the puppy to follow you, in order to imprint that you are the leader. An easy way to do this is to take the puppy outside or to a new room, set it down, and

23

then quietly walk a few steps away. The puppy may cry for a moment, but should then look for you and move toward you. Praise the puppy by picking him up and petting him. You have now offered comfort to the puppy in an otherwise frightening situation, imprinting that you provide

safety and comfort. If you already have another dog at home, this imprinting may occur with the older dog as the puppy quickly learns to follow the leader. It is a good idea to take the puppy to the potty area by himself for the first few days, in order to establish that the potty area is not for playtime.

❖ PUG POINT ❖

Housetraining

All puppies follow the same basic internal schedule. Recognizing these simple rules will help housetrain your new Pug quickly.

1. Puppies must urinate 10 to 15 minutes after each meal.

2. Puppies must have a bowel movement 15 to 30 minutes after each meal.

3. Puppies must urinate immediately after waking up.

4. Puppies must urinate any other time their activity level increases, such as playing or following the arrival of guests or family members, even if they were "just outside."

5. The more frequently a puppy is taken to the potty area in the first few weeks, the more quickly he will catch on.

6. Limiting water shortly after the evening meal may make overnight trips to the potty area less frequent.

7. Use an enzyme-type cleaner to completely remove the scent from urine and stool accidents.

Housetraining 101

Housetraining is the single most frustrating part of owning a new puppy. Ninety percent of housetraining failures are created by the owner and are the result of owners unfairly rushing a puppy and allowing too much freedom too quickly. Housetraining is relatively easy if the puppy's own schedule is followed and a few tips are used.

"Potty word": A "potty word" should be established to help your puppy learn what is expected. In a high-pitched voice, use a phrase such as *"Go potty"* as soon as you take the puppy to the potty area. Using the same doorway each time to access the area also helps create a routine.

Rewards: Each time the puppy urinates or defecates in the correct area, you must reward him.

Verbal praise as soon as the puppy begins to eliminate, followed by a small food reward or additional praise, quickly teaches the puppy what is expected. Timely verbal praise each time your puppy eliminates in the correct area is the *single most important* factor in housetraining.

Accidents: If your puppy is caught having an accident, startle him by making noise, quickly take him to the appropriate area, repeat the potty phrase, and praise him as he finishes. It is necessary to accompany your puppy to the potty area each time, until your puppy eliminates almost immediately with little or no verbal encouragement.

Walking: If your puppy is slow in eliminating, a short walk will help stimulate the process. Do *not* play with your puppy until after the task has been accomplished.

Age: There is a misconception that puppies should be housetrained by a specific age. In reality, a Pug is not completely housetrained until he has gone 8 to 12 weeks without having a single accident when given access to only one room. For many Pugs, this is not accomplished until adulthood. Females seem to take longer to housetrain than their male counterparts, and it is not uncommon to hear complaints of Pugs having accidents well after their first birthday.

Crate-Training Basics

Using a crate is the easiest, safest way to confine a puppy and significantly decreases the amount of time it takes to housetrain a Pug. The use of a crate creates a comfort zone for your puppy and offers you a sense of security when leaving your puppy unattended. Puppies that spend time in a crate are less likely to be destructive and are easier to live with.

❖ PUG POINT ❖

Entering the Crate

To teach your Pug to enter a crate willingly, place a special treat inside, give the command "Bedtime," and place the puppy in the crate. With repetition, your Pug will quickly learn that "bedtime" means "cookie time."

Feeding your puppy in a crate reinforces the natural aversion a dog has to eliminating where it eats and sleeps. The crate is never a source of punishment, rather a "safe zone" that is off limits to children and other pets. Your puppy should be in his crate at night, while eating or sleeping, and during times when proper supervision is not possible. An interactive toy or special treat can be given to

establishing routine. Housetraining aids such as potty pads or urine-scented drops can be used to draw your puppy to the proper area. Use praise as soon as the puppy begins to show interest in the designated area.

Pugs that are paper-trained have learned that there is always something on the floor in the designated area. This visual cue often creates confusion as Pugs will often consider your throw rugs or clothes on the floor the same cue, and therefore acceptable potty areas. These lapses often become habit, leading to frustrated owners and often to Pugs looking for new homes.

Pugs that have been previously paper-trained can be transitioned to eliminate outside. This process is often lengthy, so patience is crucial to success.

the puppy during prolonged periods in the crate to avoid boredom.

A Pug's crate should not be too large, offering just enough room to stand up, turn around, and sleep comfortably. Wire crates are best in warmer climates; however, enclosed crates offer added privacy.

Paper-Training or Potty Pad Training

Paper-training is often misused and in general not recommended as a form of housetraining. While Pugs are a toy breed, most can be trained to eliminate outdoors with a little effort; however, for those in high-rise buildings or where housetraining outside may be impossible, paper-training may be the only option.

When teaching a puppy to eliminate on paper, utilizing the same spot consistently is important in

---

❖ PUG POINT ❖

Stain/Odor Control

When housetraining your Pug, it is important to have a good cleaning solution available for those mistakes that will be made. There are excellent products available that are enzymes, which break down urine and stool odors and help to remove stains. In a pinch, a vinegar and water mixture can be used.

Failure to remove the urine scent will signal to your puppy that this location is acceptable to urinate in.

By 8 weeks of age, your Pug puppy has established two preferences that affect housetraining:

Substrate Preference—What he is used to eliminating on (newspaper, concrete, or grass).

Location Preference—Where he is used to eliminating (indoors or outdoors).

• First, pick up any object indoors that can be thought of as a visual cue, including the current potty papers.
• In the new outdoor area, weigh down papers to provide the visual cue.
• Even if your Pug has been paper-trained for quite some time you must adhere to the same rules used to housetrain puppies: Take him outside to the new area and use plenty of praise when elimination occurs in the new area. Your Pug may be confused at first.
• If an accident occurs in the house, the accident may be moved outside to the new potty area to create the right scent.

Litter Box Training

Some breeders are now beginning to use litter box training when puppies are as young as 4 weeks of age. Commercial litter made specifically for puppies is now readily available. Most of these products are made from recycled newspaper or paper products. This can be a great solution for apartment dwellers or for the owner who must be gone for longer periods of time than their puppy can be expected to remain clean.

Training your Pug puppy to use a litter box is easy if the breeder has already started the process. To train your puppy to eliminate in a litter box, simply follow these steps:
• Schedule trips to the litter box. Place your puppy inside the box and give your "potty" cue. If he jumps out, simply place him back in the litter box and try again.
• Praise him quietly if he begins to sniff in the box. Reward elimination with excited praise followed by a tasty treat.
• Keep the litter box clean! Many puppies will not eliminate in the box if it is dirty. Scoop out waste at least two to three times daily.

The Stop Sound

The word "No" to most of us means that our actions are unacceptable. Unfortunately, Pugs don't understand the word "No," and this can lead to trouble as your Pug grows and begins to explore the world. The dam does not reprimand her puppies with the word "No," instead offering a sharp, harsh growl that may include a snap at the offender if her warning goes unheeded. Learning to use this "stop sound" effectively can be your best bet for correcting unwanted behaviors in your Pug puppy.

The stop sound is made with the sound, "EH," as if you were trying to clear your throat. The sound should be emitted in a quick, low tone of voice. Remember, this is like a growl, and if done properly will immediately stop the young Pug puppy from whatever activity he is involved in. This stop sound should be used in situations that require that your puppy immediately stop, and should be followed up with verbal praise as soon as the unacceptable activity is terminated.

Leash Training Your Puppy

Leashtraining a puppy is easy if you don't expect your puppy to just immediately begin to go for a long walk, and you take the time to teach acceptance of both the collar and leash before trying to make your

Pug walk. Think of leash training as teaching your puppy a great game of follow the leader, complete with food rewards! Once your puppy has become comfortable with your home and the routine, you may begin to familiarize him with a collar.

• Choose a nylon collar that is extremely lightweight (cat collars work well for this), and place it on your Pug for a short period of time while you are home and playing with him. Your puppy will probably scratch at the collar, may roll on the floor trying to get the collar off, and may refuse to move for a moment. Remove the collar after a few minutes and repeat this several times a day for a few days.

• Once your puppy no longer seems to be bothered by the collar, you can begin to introduce the leash. Repeat this procedure, attaching the leash to the collar during play to allow your puppy to feel the weight of the leash. Never leave your puppy unsupervised while the leash is dragging behind.

• After a few sessions with both the collar and the leash on, you should begin to pick up the leash and follow behind your puppy. At this point, your puppy will be walking you. Make sure to keep the leash loose so that your puppy does not learn that pulling works.

• Try to coax your puppy in your direction using food treats, your voice, clapping your hands, or whatever it may take to get the puppy going where you want him to go. If the puppy backs up, allow him to

remain at the end of the leash with the lead taut, but do not pull the puppy toward you. Most puppies quickly learn that if they go backward, they can go only so far before the lead is tightened.

• If the puppy steps forward and toward you, it brings relief from the tight leash, and this forward movement brings a verbal reward as you quickly praise him for moving in your direction.

• Try to keep this forward momentum going using lots of praise and slowly walking backward away from the puppy, but not too fast that the lead becomes tight and gives a negative impression of the forward movement. The relief of moving forward on a loose lead, combined with the positive reinforcement of praise and treats quickly teaches the Pug

puppy that walking with you is the way to go!

The "Struggling Catch Me" Game

As your Pug puppy becomes a bit older, it will become comfortable with a bit of independence. Pug puppies between the ages of 12 weeks and 6 months often try to pinpoint their boundaries and then attempt to see how far they can push them. An adolescent Pug's favorite game is "The Chase," better known as "My owner is too slow to catch me." Unfortunately, the owner inadvertently reinforces this behavior every time she gives chase and is unsuccessful in capturing her Pug. Teaching a puppy to come when called can eliminate this frustrating game. With the help of a family member or friend, we can quickly turn this game around and teach the Pug to chase us.

The object of the "struggling catch me" game is to make your puppy want to chase and ultimately catch you. Ask someone to hold your puppy while he is standing and then walk a few steps in front. Turn around and get your puppy's attention. You can say his name, make funny sounds, jump up and down—whatever is needed to get your puppy excited. When your puppy is frantically trying to get away from being held, say his name and then the command, "*Here.*" The helper should release the puppy on this command. Quickly move backward away from your now streaking puppy, stop, and let the puppy catch you. Bend down and praise the puppy by petting him, give a treat, and tell him, "*What a smart puppy*!" You have now taught your puppy that chasing you is a lot of fun and at the same time, taught him to come when called. Practice this game often to continually reinforce this important behavior.

Socializing Your Puppy

Shortly after your puppy arrives home, it is time to think about creating new experiences. A puppy that is allowed to meet new challenges and succeeds in mastering each one becomes a well-adjusted, happy adult.

Kindergarten puppy training is the most effective way to help your Pug experience new people, environments, and objects. It is taught between the ages of two months and five months, using only positive reinforcement. The ideal time to begin this class is between 10 and 12 weeks of age.

A well-run puppy kindergarten class provides socialization with people and other puppies as well as exposure to novel objects

and sounds. It also begins to teach puppy manners and foundational obedience behaviors in a safe and secure location. The American Veterinary Society of Animal Behavior recommends that all puppies join this type of class as soon as they have received one set of vaccinations from a veterinarian. Waiting to socialize until your puppy is fully vaccinated poses a behavioral risk that is now believed to be far greater than the risk of disease in a well-managed class.

Socialization is allowing your Pug puppy to meet new people and experience new places outside of class. If a weekly puppy class is not available, you may create opportunities to socialize your puppy on your own. Short trips to children's sporting events or the store become great classrooms for a Pug puppy. Strangers will gladly give your Pug a small treat while they pet him, teaching the puppy acceptance of unfamiliar hands. Backyard play equipment can become confidence-building tools as puppies learn to go up and down stairs or slides, or through tunnels. Socialization also means introducing your puppy to other well-vaccinated, familiar dogs. Choose your puppy's play partners carefully, as you want all experiences to be positive! Dog parks and large pet stores are not wise choices for early socialization. The unknown vaccination status of unfamiliar dogs in these locations may put your puppy at risk for contracting disease. Some of these dogs are also not well

socialized with puppies and could injure your puppy. Approach any new activity in a positive manner and reward often to create a fun learning experience. The success your puppy achieves early in life will help to minimize the effects of stressful events as an adult.

The American Kennel Club (AKC) Star Puppy Program

One of the best ways to accomplish all of your training goals is to enroll in a puppy class that follows the recommendations of the AKC Star Puppy Program. This program was designed to help educate the new puppy owner on how to be a responsible owner as well as teach your Pug puppy all of the foundational skills for becoming a well-behaved adult. Instructors who offer the Star Puppy program will help ensure that your Pug puppy is socialized with other puppies in a safe environment, is exposed to novel sights and sounds in a positive manner, and learns basic obedience skills. It is a great way to make sure that your Pug has a solid foundation of good behavior.

Chapter Four

Preventing Problem Pugs

Pugs have a great fondness for mischief and they possess an uncanny ability to charm their owners once they have discovered trouble. Pug owners often put up with lapses in behavior, even offering excuses for recurrent bad behavior. This tolerance on behalf of the owner creates habits that soon become intolerable behaviors. The most common behavioral problems can be prevented as long as the Pug owner identifies the unwanted behavior early and is willing to discipline those otherwise angelic Pugs.

Housetraining Issues

Housetraining problems make up the highest number of behavioral complaints when dealing with Pugs. In nearly every case involving an adult Pug that has repeated accidents in the home, the diagnosis of "incomplete housetraining" can be made. Incomplete housetraining is the end result of the Pug owner's failure to be disciplined in teaching proper house manners while her Pug was still a puppy. One or two accidents occur each day, or the owner has tolerated weekly "mistakes," often when her young Pug was offered too much unsupervised freedom. Those lapses stretch into more accidents, especially when the now adult Pug is alone or when it is too cold outside, or raining too hard, or just too wet for little Pug feet. These excuses are used to justify why that otherwise perfect puppy has suddenly become an adult with a problem.

Incomplete housetraining can be prevented. The Pug owner cannot overlook those "little lapses." Pug owners must restrict unsupervised access in the home of any Pug that does not earn freedom by demonstrating perfect housetraining habits. Each Pug has different limitations on how much freedom he can enjoy. It is strictly up to the owner to recognize how often her Pug needs to visit the potty area, and to determine what factors may overstimulate her Pug and cause a breakdown in housetraining. Remember that successful housetraining means constant supervision, frequent successful trips to the acceptable potty area, and strict confinement in the owner's absence.

Marking

Marking behavior, also known as leg lifting, can also be a problem in Pugs. This behavior is usually associated with unneutered male Pugs; however, females that are not spayed, and young, adolescent Pugs that reside in multidog households may also be at risk. Pug owners often proclaim that their Pug is "mad at them" or "acting out" each time a urine accident occurs on such items as furniture legs, corners of walls, and draperies or vertical blinds. The fact of the matter is that leg lifting on indoor objects is not the result of spite or frustration. In unaltered male and female Pugs, hormones are the catalyst for leg lifting. Intact males store a large amount of testosterone in their muscle tissue at all times upon reaching maturity. This hormone triggers a dog's natural instinct to mark his territory by urinating on upright, prominent places. Pugs are no exception, as they believe that every square inch of any room in which they visit ultimately belongs to them. In many instances, neutering the adult Pug helps to decrease marking behavior significantly within six to eight weeks following the surgery.

Dominant female Pugs, those girls that are bossy and overbearing, may also exhibit marking behavior, particularly in multi-Pug households. Unlike their male counterparts, female Pugs usually mark objects on the floor such as clothing, shoes, toys, and rugs. These accidents are generally small dribbles of urine, just enough to let others know that they were there. Spaying can help to decrease this annoyance in adult female Pugs. A belly band or male diaper may be helpful in changing the naughty boy who lifts his leg indoors. A sanitary pad can be used inside the band, which soaks up any urine, leaving your furniture clean and dry. Many Pugs find wearing a wet belly band unpleasant, and this may deter them from marking indoors. Over a length of time the band can often be removed as the behavior diminishes. Likewise, diapers or "panties" can be useful in reducing the marking of a female Pug.

Bladder Infections

Recurring urine accidents may also be an indication of a bladder infection or the symptom of an underlying medical condition. If urine accidents are suddenly frequent, or have just recently become a problem, your Pug should be taken to your veterinarian for an examination.

Retraining

Adult Pugs that exhibit housetraining lapses can be successfully retrained but the success cannot be achieved without the owner's commitment to constant supervision, or strict confinement during the owner's absence. Again, the use of the crate becomes a significant part of the housetraining process whenever the owner cannot provide adequate supervision. Pug owners will find that if they treat these adults as if they were puppies, cleanliness in the house is reestablished much more quickly.

• To begin the retraining process, restrict the Pug's access to one or two rooms in which constant supervision is possible.

• When there have been no accidents in the designated room(s) over an 8- to 12-week period, add access to an additional adjacent room.

• If your Pug begins to have accidents again, take away the access to the new area.

• If, after several weeks, your Pug is still accident-free you may then add another additional adjacent room.

• Step by step, room-by-room, the Pug begins to learn that accidents should not occur.

It is also important when retraining these adults that a schedule be established and adhered to as closely as possible once again until the Pug has completed 8 to 12 weeks without a single accident in the house.

Accident Areas

The owners of "naughty Pugs" should accompany them each time to the potty area, in order to praise them immediately when the correct behavior of eliminating occurs. It is also equally important to make frequently used accident areas unavailable or unattractive until the offender is accident-free. Closing doors or

using dog gates may be necessary to completely restrict access to other areas while you are in the process of retraining your Pug. Any area that has previously been used as a potty spot indoors should be treated with a urine neutralizer to prevent a recurrence of the improper use of the area.

Patience

Any Pug that an owner determines has never been completely trustworthy—has never gone eight weeks without a potty accident— must earn independence through accident-free time. This unfortunately includes many Pugs adopted through rescue organizations. In many cases, the retraining results in completely unsupervised access, but this may take several months or even years and can be a true test of patience on the part of the owner. It is important to remember when reteaching house habits to the adult Pug that there are no "quick fixes" or "magic remedies" for success, only the owner's patience, understanding, determination, and commitment to retraining in what can be a very difficult task.

Destructive Chewing

Dogs have a natural tendency and desire to chew. Pugs are no exception. Pug puppies, in particular, find molding and furniture legs particularly attractive and an excellent substitution for those store-bought chew toys. Many Pugs also find electrical cords are fun to chew—a potentially deadly situation. The majority of destructive chewing episodes occur in young Pugs that are left unsupervised for a period of time. Until

your Pug learns what is acceptable to chew, supervision is the key to preventing tragic accidents and injuries. Once again, a crate or playpen keeps your Pug safe from chewing hazards and saves you money by safeguarding household belongings when supervision is not possible.

Boredom

Boredom is the most common cause of destructive chewing. Remember, Pugs love mischief and have a unique gift in their ability to create their own fun activities. Toys and puzzles that are considered interactive have recently become available for dogs and are a "must have" for any new Pug owner. These toys all reward the dog for playing with them by randomly dropping food treats when picked up, pushed, or rolled repeatedly. To a Pug, any toy that produces a food reward is

worth playing with! Other objects such as vegetable-based chew bones, bully sticks, cow hooves, and rawhide bones may become suitable boredom busters if they are the appropriate size for a Pug. The challenge for the Pug owner is to continually find acceptable toys that the Pug will utilize as outlets for activity and energy. Constructive play minimizes boredom, which, in turn, decreases the likelihood of destructive chewing.

A brisk 15-minute walk twice daily can be a tremendous help in channeling your Pug's energy, as well as preventing weight gain and obesity.

Boundary Training— to Fence or Not to Fence

The significant number of Pugs turning up in shelters and unclaimed by their owners illustrates the fact that many Pugs are not homebodies. Pugs find other animals, children, and people, in general, amusing and delight in wandering off in an attempt to befriend each and every one. Pug-proofing your home must include a provision to secure your yard, either by a fence or some other method of confinement.

Fenced Yards

A fenced yard provides a safe area for your Pug to enjoy activities such as bird-watching, squirrel chasing and sunbathing. Fences also help to deter individuals who may otherwise attempt to steal unsupervised Pugs, a disturbing trend that seems to be increasing in some areas of the United States.

The type of fence used to protect your Pug is really a matter of individual preference; however, many Pugs seem to be driven to find the best way under, around, over, or through the boundary. To help discourage would-be "Houdini Pugs," make sure that there are no gaps or openings along the bottom of the fence. Wooden fences should be inspected regularly for loose boards, and objects that can be climbed upon or used to catapult over low fences should be moved a safe distance away from the fence. While the physical boundary of a fence provides the Pug owner with a sense of security, determined Pugs may find unique ways to escape if they are left unsupervised for any length of time.

Containment Fence Systems

For some Pug owners, a fence is not practical or possible. Under-

ground containment systems, also known as electric or invisible fencing systems, can be an acceptable alternative method of controlling a Pug's outdoor boundaries.

New technologies have made these systems more affordable and much easier to install. Above-ground systems can also be purchased and installed easily by the majority of Pug owners. Whether the system is professionally installed or set up by the Pug owner, the key to success in trusting this system is in the training of the Pug to respect the electronic boundary.

Each fencing system utilizes a radio signal that is sent throughout the system's boundary. The boundary consists of a wire buried below the ground at the appropriate spot, or a series of posts placed a short distance apart along the designated boundary line. A small receiver collar is worn by the Pug, which picks up the signal from the boundary system whenever the Pug enters the warning zone. The warning zone in most systems is adjustable to fit the specific area. The average distance is 4 to 5 feet (122–152 cm) from the actual boundary. An audible, high-pitched warning beep is emitted when the Pug enters the warning zone, cautioning him from moving any farther forward. For those Pugs that need an additional warning, moving further toward the boundary brings an uncomfortable electric shock that can be adjusted by the owner to fit the degree of needs of her Pug.

It is important for all Pugs to understand and respect their home boundaries. Fences provide a clear visual boundary, while using an electric containment system provides no clear visual sign. Training a Pug to respect a containment fence system begins with a series of markers placed along the boundary as a visual aid. The Pug soon learns to associate the visual cue of the markers with the audible beep, which precedes the unpleasant shock.

Teaching Outdoor Boundaries

Properly teaching outdoor boundaries to a young Pug involves separating the learning process into two parts: learning where the boundary is, and learning to quickly return to the safety of the yard. Any Pug that does not come immediately when called will soon learn that he does not have to heed the boundary of the yard. To help your Pug learn the boundary, use a marker system to help teach where the end of the yard is. Place utility flags or some other form of visual markers along the boundary, evenly spaced, no more than 5 feet (152 cm) apart. In order to teach your Pug to return to the safety of the yard, the recall is taught.

• Place your Pug on a leash of at least 6 feet (183 cm) in length (retractable leashes work great for this exercise), and walk toward the boundary.

• When your Pug reaches within 5 feet (152 cm) of the boundary, call his name followed by the word "*Here*," and give a short, quick tug on the leash toward you if needed.

• Walk quickly backwards away from the boundary and praise your Pug for following.

• Stop and let your Pug catch you and praise, praise, praise! A food treat should be given at this time to reinforce the idea that your Pug has moved away from the boundary.

• Repeat this exercise several times each day over a period of time, and before you know it, your Pug will respect the visual boundary of those markers. Once you are certain that he understands where the boundary is, remove every other marker. After a period of time, the remaining markers may be removed if the Pug continues to respect the boundary.

Note: It is important to note that not every Pug will learn to respect boundaries if there is no actual fence. Some Pugs find that while there is "no place like home," there are too many other interesting things waiting "over the rainbow" (or on the other side of the street). For these Pugs, the only safe option is to have him on a leash at all times.

The Barker

Pugs have never really been thought of as great watchdogs; however, many have earned the reputation as exceptional noisemakers. First, we must understand that not all barking is bad or inappropriate. Barking is a normal form of communication among dogs. Each dog has its own series of barking sequences that can be used in a variety of situations. High-pitched barks often indicate excitement, happiness, or playtime, and most Pugs happily "woo-woo" when greeting their owners. Barking is your Pug's attempt to communicate with you and the clear announcement to the world in general that a Pug has arrived and must be dealt with. Learning to read your Pug's attempts to communicate can be quite amusing. To a Pug, any and all barking is appropriate. It is our duty as owners to identify when barking is inappropriate, and to correct uncontrolled barking when necessary.

Pugs learn to bark at a very early age, emitting small, sharp barks as early as 21 days of age. Barking begins to signal excitement as the mother approaches, frustration when a littermate has taken away a toy, and anxiety when faced with an unfamiliar object or situation. Sequences of barking are normal canine behavior for a Pug puppy, and are easily tolerated by the Pug owner. As a Pug becomes more independent and begins to feel more comfortable with his surroundings, the normal canine behavior of territorial defense begins to surface. Some Pugs take this job very seriously. When a visitor approaches the front door, most Pug owners appreciate a warning bark. In some cases, the barking sequence may change as the visitor approaches the door. The communication begins as a low bark, with or without growling, and may change to a high-pitched, rapid barking sequence signaling your Pug's overwhelming joy that a new friend has arrived at the front door. When in communicating this joy the barking becomes unstoppable, or when the desire to protect his own boundaries causes constant vocalization, the Pug must be taught that the behavior is not appropriate.

Correcting the Behavior

There are two steps to correcting inappropriate barking. The first step is to interrupt the barking sequence. One of the most effective ways is to use a shaker can, which can be created by placing a few coins or small rocks in an empty soda can and taping the end closed with duct tape. This tool, when shaken or tossed to the floor, startles the barking Pug and momentarily stops the barking. It is at this precise moment of quiet that the second step is initiated: rewarding correct behavior when your Pug is quiet. The timing of the interruption and the use of treats and praise are critical to minimizing and eliminating unwanted barking behavior. The interruption must occur during the actual uncontrolled barking sequence, not following the behavior. Treating your Pug immediately when the barking stops reinforces that you are pleased with his quiet moments.

Reasons for Barking

Activity outside windows: As many Pugs attempt to survey the world around them, their favorite lookout points often include furniture in front of windows. Pug owners often report that their Pugs are constantly barking at activity that occurs outside the house. The frequency of the barking, as well as the pitch of the barking sequence, will give you insight into what your Pug is trying to communicate. Access to these favorite spots may need to be limited, especially if the barking is a problem while the owner is away from home and the neighbors are continuously reminded that a Pug resides next door.

One of the best ways to change the Pug who is always "on alert" at windows is to take away what he wants as soon as the barking begins— access to the view. With consistent practice of the following sequence, your Pug will quickly learn to bark and then be quiet on command.

1. Wait until your Pug is barking and then quickly but quietly approach him. When you are near, give the warning cue "*Quiet*" and quickly draw the curtains or lower the shades.

2. Walk away without saying another word.

3. The curtains should remain closed for two to three minutes. You may then open them and wait to see if the barking begins again. In the initial stages of this behavior modification, it is almost certain to happen again. Simply repeat the process when your Pug begins to patrol again.

For this use of "negative punishment" to be effective, you must also prevent your Pug from barking out the window in your absence. Wax paper, artificial stained glass appliqués, or butcher paper may be needed to control your Pug's view of the world when you are not home.

Intruders: Pugs also enjoy spending time outdoors in warm, sunny weather. It is not uncommon for them to announce their presence to the entire neighborhood by barking at each intruder, be it bird, squirrel, car, or paper blowing in the breeze. Pug owners often ignore these barking episodes, a mistake which they soon begin to regret.

Barking episodes that occur at a distance from the owner can be extremely difficult to control, as interruption cannot be correctly timed, and praise is often forgotten or not given in a timely manner. Yelling at your Pug from inside the house is a mistake. This only seems to convince him that you are joining the attempt to ward off the intruder, and he often increases the barking. A strong recall, or being able to call your Pug to come inside when he is barking, is often the only way to eliminate this type of barking.

No-Bark Collars

The most common tool used to silence the barker is a no-bark collar. No-bark collars can be found in the form of electronic or "shock-type" collars, spray-type collars, and collars that emit an unpleasant, high-pitched sound. All of these collars create an unpleasant circumstance when the barking sequence continues unabated, creating an aversion to uninterrupted barking. While these collars are readily available and can be effective, the Pug owner who is unfamiliar with these types of aversive correction methods should

exercise great care when first using them, especially when training with shock-type collars. A correction that is incorrectly timed or delivered at an intensity that is too painful or extremely uncomfortable can create a Pug that is now afraid to go to the area where the correction occurred.

Lemon Juice

Well-intentioned individuals may suggest lemon juice, squirted in the Pug's mouth during a barking sequence, as a means for controlling barking of all types. Many trainers still advocate the use of spray bottles or lemon juice, but it can be quite difficult to ensure that the juice will indeed enter only the Pug's mouth and not the nose and eyes as well.

Barking in Young Pugs

Pugs are, by nature, friendly, easygoing, and quite accepting of other dogs and animals. The most common barking misbehaviors occur in young Pugs, especially those that have not had the benefits of proper socialization. These Pugs often bark uncontrollably when on a leash, in situations where other dogs are present, such as the veterinarian's waiting room. This type of barking in Pugs is often due to either a lack of self-control in the adolescent Pug who loves everyone and is frustrated that he cannot visit, or a defensive, fear-based response that indicates he would really like to be left alone. Pug owners often unknowingly encourage this behavior by reinforcing it as they pet their Pug. In an effort to reassure the Pug that everything is okay, the owner verbally praises the barker, even picking up their noisy Pug. Each stroke of the owner's hand and "It's okay" that the Pug hears from the owner convinces the barker that you are pleased and that he should continue barking. The key to changing this type of behavior is to determine whether your Pug wants to say "hi" or wants to leave the room. His body language may offer some clues to help you decide how to best handle the barking. Is his tail still curled tightly over his body or has it become lost, hanging partial down, which signals fear? Is his body stiff during the barking or is he loose and bouncy, often moving his rear end side to side as he wiggles with excitement?

Here are some ways to help him learn that silence is golden:

• Try redirecting his focus using treats. Wave a tasty treat in front of his nose and then move it back toward you. If your Pug's attention moves even slightly in your direction, REWARD! You will need to continue to reward your Pug's attention frequently at first. If he is social, and the other dog or person is also friendly and can be safely approached, you can give your Pug the command "*Free*" and let him visit briefly as long as you time it to coincide with when he is quiet.

• Give the verbal cue "*Quiet*" and move farther away from the dog or person he is barking at. If your Pug is worried, this increased distance may help him feel safer and may decrease or eliminate further barking. If his barking is due to his "social butterfly" status, he will quickly learn that barking moves him farther away from the very thing he wants. If he remains quiet you can praise him and simply move a step or two closer. Treats can also be given as a bonus reward for continued quiet behavior. A key component to solving the on-leash barking problem is to praise your Pug as soon as the barking stops and he remains quiet.

No matter what the circumstance is, when a Pug becomes a chronic barker, it is the owner who ultimately allows reinforcement of the barking behavior, or is determined to eliminate this annoying habit. The Pug's vocal ability comes naturally and helps to add to his charm. Don't allow uncontrolled barking to detract from his wonderful personality.

Here Kitty-Kitty — the Cat Chaser

It is the nature of a Pug to want to conjure up fun. Adult Pugs often find their feline housemates to be rather boring and uninteresting, opting for other excitement. Young and adolescent Pugs, however, do not understand the nature of the cat's routinely dormant activity, and delight in trying to change the feline lifestyle. For these Pugs, any movement by the cat, however small, elicits the urge to torment and chase the unsuspecting and unamused kitty.

For the household with multiple pets, the balance of power should be decided by those pets that interact on a regular basis. It is the cat that must deliver the first correction to the instigating Pug, particularly if the Pug is a young puppy attempting to learn his place in the multipet household. A few quick paw swipes from an unhappy cat will teach the curious Pug puppy who is going to be the boss. While most cats don't use their claws when interacting with a puppy, one word of caution—if your cat has not been declawed, it is a good idea to keep your cat's nails trimmed to avoid any accidental scratches to your puppy's eyes. Cats that are allowed to stand up to a young Pug rarely have to deal with a chronic kitty chaser.

Intervening

For those cats that will not stand up to an overzealous Pug, or are unable to deliver a strong message due to advanced age, the owner must intervene on the cat's behalf. Pugs often telescope their mischievous thoughts by focusing intently on the cat, bringing their ears high up on their head and very forward,

quivering in anticipation and snorting a short warning. These signals are usually in combination with a very upright and forward body posture, as the "killer Pug" gets ready to initiate the chase. It is at this point that the Pug owner should attempt to focus the Pug's attention elsewhere, by using a verbal command that the Pug already knows. Call him by name, and if the response is to turn or look at you, praise quickly and call him to you using a high-pitched, excited tone of voice. Remember, at this point you will need to appear more attractive than the fun your Pug associates with chasing the cat, so make some noise and let your Pug know that by coming to you there will be a great reward! Keep treats handy nearby or in your pocket so you can quickly offer a food reward, which will often be enough to convince your naughty Pug that you hold a better option than chasing the cat. The object is to use your voice and body language to prevent the chase. The tastier the treats, the less your Pug will want to return his attention to the cat. Once the chase has already begun, it is much more difficult to stop the behavior, as you are not nearly as fun and interesting as pinning that kitty to the floor!

There will be times when the owner cannot gain her Pug's attention, as the excitement of the subsequent chase is so great that no amount of owner antics will prevent an all-out Pug and kitty marathon. For these Pugs some other method must be used to stop the chase behavior. Interrupting the chase can be difficult, as so often the Pug is unable to divert attention to anything other than the panicked, shrieking cat. A shaker can may be thrown near the Pug to momentarily startle him (and probably the cat, too), giving the owner a window of opportunity to intervene and refocus the Pug's attention. Squirt guns or plant-spray bottles may also be effective. Whatever method you use, praise and treats must be given the instant your Pug stops the chase and turns his attention to you. Reinforce your Pug's correct behavior to help bring about the understanding that you offer a better alternative to cat chasing.

Changing the Behavior

A very small number of Pugs, particularly adults that have had no previous exposure to cats and are subsequently placed in households with young cats, need a physical correction to begin to learn to ignore cats. A collar and leash prove the tools necessary to begin teaching.

• Begin by using a 4-foot (122 cm) leash attached to a simple buckle collar.

• Walk your Pug near the cat and if the Pug shows little or no interest in the cat, give praise and treats to

reinforce the correct behavior of ignoring the cat. Continue to reward your Pug for remaining focused on you, or for each time his focus is directed at the cat and then quickly returns to you.

• Give your Pug a release cue of "Free" and walk your Pug away from the cat. Return again for another try.

• If, at any time, your Pug attempts to chase the cat or shows a focused interest in the kitty, give a slight jerk toward you on the leash and call your Pug's name as you move away from the cat. When he focuses on you or looks away from the cat, quickly give praise and a food reward.

• Repetition of these corrections and praise over a period of time will condition your Pug to ignore the cat and eagerly look to you, the owner, for praise and attention.

Most Pugs that habitually chase their feline housemates can be taught to coexist peacefully, but a very small percentage of Pugs may never be good companions for cats, and may require constant supervision by the owner whenever the cat is present.

The Aggressive Pug

Aggressive Pugs just can't possibly exist, right? The Pug has always been bred as a companion dog where temperament is an important characteristic. Aggression can exist in any breed, but it is important to understand that any form of aggression from a Pug is atypical. Aggression is a complex behavioral problem, and often has multiple underlying factors and a variety of causes.

Aggression is often a learned behavior, the result of poor socialization, or the end result of a dog with an intense fear response. Behavioral specialists attempt to classify the type or types of aggression that a dog exhibits before formulating a treatment plan.

When dealing with an aggressive Pug, it is important to first determine if there may be an underlying medical cause that is triggering the aggression, such as an underactive thyroid gland (hypothyroidism) or previously undiagnosed pain or neurological disease. Prompt treatment of any medical problem may decrease the incidence of aggression. If no medical component can be identified, careful examination of the situations where aggression occurs may offer clues as to the triggers of aggression and ultimately offer some insight into possible treatment options. It is important to note that an aggressive episode from your Pug can result in injuries to family members, guests, and other animals. To avoid being bitten use caution. It is advisable to seek help from your veterinarian or a trained behavioral professional for any type of aggression, especially when the bite is directed at a human.

Multidog Households

We are fortunate that when most owners discuss aggression in Pugs, they are usually referring to Pugs that fight with other dogs, or interdog aggression. Normal canine behavior involves some posturing or positioning among the dogs in a household or family group. Pugs living in multiple-dog households may identify a dominant or leader dog. Each canine member has a place or ranking position within the group, which is respected by those dogs whose position is beneath it. It is natural for multiple-Pug households to encounter some squabbles within the canine family group, especially if there is a young Pug that is attempting to strengthen his position within the group, or an older Pug whose authority is easily challenged by a stronger, younger Pug.

The Owner's Role

The dynamics of living in a multi-dog household require the owner to be a solid, calm presence. Most Pugs do not wish to assume the role of the leader, as this takes far more energy than snoozing on the couch or chewing on a favorite toy. A Pug owner who establishes consistent routines for feeding, and who teaches self-control through positive reinforcement of good Pug behaviors such as "sit" or "wait," often has little or no squabbling among housemates. Their Pugs are focused on receiving rewards from "mom" following her lead, instead of wasting energy battling each other.

Daily training sessions using positive reinforcement and clear expectations for behavior at mealtimes, putting a leash on your Pug, or gaining access to the outdoors are often all that is needed to decrease or eliminate aggression between dogs living in the same household.

As a Pug owner, it is completely normal to want to see a hierarchy established based on which Pug has lived in a household the longest. If all of the dogs in a household or family group are Pugs, the owner should make every effort to allow

---

❖ PUG POINT ❖

Aggression/Submission

Signs of aggression include
1. Ears held high on head, tail straight up, and hackles may be raised.
2. Growling, snarling
3. Refusal to give up toys
4. Growling over food and toys

Signs of submission include
1. Low ear set, relaxed body posture
2. Licking and whining
3. Rolling over onto back
4. Relinquishing toys and food willingly

---

the housemates to establish their own hierarchy. Unfortunately, the oldest Pug or the biggest Pug may not always be the leader. If your Pug resides in a household that includes multiple breeds of dogs, especially if there is a great size difference between the dogs, you may need to carefully intervene during a squabble to ensure the safety of your Pug. Intervention must be done in such a way that the owner does not upset the social structure that is already present.

In every home where multiple dogs reside, the owner should try to identify the social structure of their "Pug Pack." Observe your Pugs in play, during feeding times, and when toys or treats are present. Is there one Pug that always takes the best toys? Does one Pug always go outside before his housemates? Can you identify which Pug always licks the faces of the others? Dominant or leader Pugs may be the first to do things. Pugs in a position of leadership enjoy all the best toys, are allowed to take toys away from others whenever they choose to, and are constantly having their face washed by their housemates. Conversely, subordinate Pugs roll over in front of the leader Pug, dole out kisses to their superior as a gesture of goodwill, and sit by quietly while the controlling Pug moves from toy to toy.

Once the owner knows which Pug is considered to be the leader by its housemates, every attempt should be made to reinforce the hierarchy that has already been established. If the owner can continually reinforce the routines already in place and respected by the Pugs themselves, aggressive episodes among the Pugs should decrease in frequency and intensity, as the Pugs no longer feel the need to constantly reassert themselves. As the multiple-Pug household changes, either with the addition or loss of a Pug, the dynamics of that household hierarchy may change as well. It is up to the owners to quickly observe any changes in the social structure and adapt their behavior to accommodate the new hierarchy.

Pug owners often report that inter-Pug aggression is more frequent, and the episodes are much more intense when the battles are among females. Their male counterparts, which happily relinquish the leader role, often consider female Pugs dominant.

When Good Pugs Go Bad

Aggression toward other Pugs in the same household may have one or more additional components. Territorial aggression, such as protecting a crate or a piece of furniture from his housemates, may spark a contest. Each Pug believes that he has his own "space" that needs to be respected by others around him. For some Pugs this space is very small, less than a foot (30 cm) or two. For others, this space can be exceptionally large, with the Pug in question claiming ownership of a space as large as an entire room. If the perceived space requirement is violated, a fight may ensue. Possessive aggression, the protection of an object from others, also causes a significant amount of inter-Pug fights.

A Pug that has had the benefit of the interacting with its littermates during the critical social developmental period of six to eight weeks of age is significantly less likely to exhibit territorial or possessive aggression. These Pugs also understand the concept of the social hierarchy, and tend to accept their role and position much more quickly when introduced to a new household or housemate.

Aggression Toward Humans

Very few Pugs ever exhibit aggression in any form toward a human. When a Pug does attempt to bite his owner or another human, your first reaction may be to laugh at this flat-faced demon that has taken possession of your little angel, or make excuses for the unusual behavior.

The reality is that any dog bite is a frightening experience and should be taken very seriously. It is highly recommended that the owner of any Pug with a history of aggression toward people seek professional counseling from a veterinarian or a trained behavioral specialist.

Possessive aggression: Possessive aggression is perhaps the most common form of aggression involved when a Pug bites. Unfortunately, many of the bites involving a Pug are directed toward children who unknowingly trigger the bite by playing with a toy that the Pug considers his own or venture too closely to a food dish, which, of course, the Pug considers the center of the universe. The owner of a possessive-aggressive Pug must know and understand the limitations that occur in these situations. The owner may either choose to always avoid situations that may provoke aggression, or attempt to countercondition the Pug to willingly give up the object(s) that trigger a bite.

Avoidance is often the easiest solution to prevent aggression associated with an overpossessive Pug. The owner may simply choose to avoid the very thing that causes the Pug to bite. This might include eliminating access to rawhide bones or other objects that trigger an aggressive response, feeding the food-aggressive Pug in a crate or other isolated area, or keeping the Pug away from children when toys are present or supervision is impossible.

Counterconditioning: Counterconditioning involves teaching the possessive Pug to "give up" the coveted object in favor of a food reward or other acceptable object. This process takes time and effort, so avoidance may be necessary in combination with retraining until the possessive behavior is eliminated or significantly decreased. To begin the counterconditioning process, choose a key word such as "*Give*" or "*Drop it*." Using an item that does not cause the Pug to react aggressively, allow the Pug to chew on it or play with it. While the Pug has some physical contact with the object, say the key word in a strong tone of voice and immediately put the food reward in front of the Pug. When the Pug takes the food, verbally praise him. When the Pug has learned to immediately release that object upon the command word, begin the process again with an object that initiates a stronger possessive response. The Pug should be given the release command when in possession of the item and immediately receive a food reward and verbal praise when the item is released. If the item is not relinquished on command, or the Pug responds in an aggressive manner, continue to practice avoidance and consult with your veterinarian or a professional trainer who can help.

Most types of aggression can be fueled by the presence of hormones. The peaks of both testosterone and estrogen can increase the intensity and frequency of aggression. Any Pug that exhibits aggressive behavior should be spayed or neutered.

Chapter Five
Pre-Owned Pugs

For many people, today's hectic lifestyle has made raising and training a puppy impractical or nearly impossible. The cost of purchasing a Pug puppy may make owning a Pug out of reach for others. Fortunately, there are often adult Pugs, young and old, that for some reason are in search of a new home.

Pugs seem to be quite adaptable when faced with adjusting to a new home. Most enter a new household with great enthusiasm. It takes only a short time before an adult Pug realizes that he has now become the boss of this new home, and who the pushovers in the new family are. Within a few weeks, the Pug is at home in his new environment, enjoying each day like royalty.

Several options exist for adding an adult Pug to your family. These options should be explored carefully to find the best one for you.

Adoption Through Breed Rescue

All across the United States dedicated Pug lovers have come together to provide temporary homes for Pugs in need. These groups work only with Pugs, providing medical care, behavioral counseling, and socialization for the foster Pugs in their care. Veterinary bills can be extremely high for foster caregivers as many of these unwanted Pugs have had minimal, if any, previous medical care and are in need of vaccinations, parasite control, and routine dental care. Most rescue groups charge a nominal fee to adopt a Pug in an effort to maintain funds for the next Pug that needs to be fostered.

The steady stream of adult Pugs looking for new homes through breed rescue has many wondering where they all come from. The reasons for displacement are as varied as the Pugs themselves. The vast majority are given up due to behavioral issues resulting from a lack of socialization or absence of training as a puppy. Still others are wanderers, ending up as strays in shelters. Most of these are male Pugs that are not neutered and became lost while in search of a girlfriend. The long list of chronic health problems in the Pug, along with the sometimes high cost of treating these problems, makes up a large percentage of the Pugs seeking new homes through breed rescue. The popularity of Pugs

with senior citizens leads to a large number of older Pugs seeking new homes, as assisted living becomes a necessity for their aging owners.

Breed rescue organizations began to emerge in the early 1980s. Within the past 20 years, nearly every breed has at least some form of rescue program, tirelessly working to place each and every dog that comes into the program. Many of these organizations are associated with local clubs, staffed by dedicated breeders. Others are simply Pug owners who have come together because they truly love the breed and wish to help those dogs less fortunate than their own. There are, however, individuals who claim to be part of "rescue groups" that operate without regard for the best interests of the dogs they foster.

Reputable Breed Rescue Programs

Reputable breed rescue programs never ask for money in excess of their normal adoption fee "up front." Some rescue organizations may hold onto the adoption fee until a suitable Pug is available; however, most do not require any down payment as they cannot guarantee that a Pug will become available. Those breed rescue organization that are reputable work with various shelters or humane societies in their area, and are recommended by local veterinarians, obedience trainers, and kennel clubs. Educating the public and limiting the number of Pugs needing homes in the future is a priority of every breed rescue. With this in mind, responsible breed rescue groups never place Pugs that are not spayed or neutered unless accompanied by a spay/neuter agreement, which must be returned upon completion of the surgery. Reputable Pug rescue groups do follow-up calls, so be prepared!

Evaluating Each Pug

Pug rescue groups are well organized throughout this country, with many sharing information on Pugs as well as prospective owners. In many cases, a rescue group may cover more than one state, making it necessary to make a short trip to see if you wish to adopt a Pug. While adult Pugs easily fit into many home situations, the majority of Pugs seeking new homes have very specific requirements or special needs. Pug rescue organizations do an excellent job of evaluating each Pug that they receive, in order to permanently place him in the ideal situation. Rescue volunteers care for homeless Pugs in their homes, evaluating compatibility and training issues, and pinpointing any specific needs that the Pug may have. This process of matching helps to ensure that every Pug is placed in the best suitable home. Likewise, prospective owners must be screened to better understand their lifestyle, family situation, and ability to care for that special Pug.

Application: The first step in adopting a Pug through rescue is to fill out an application with the rescue group. Applications vary from one organization to the next, but every form contains questions that will obtain the same information about

the prospective adopting family. When filling out each application, it is important to answer all the questions honestly to provide information that will ultimately result in matching you with the right Pug for your family's lifestyle.

The home visit: The next phase of adoption may be a home visit from a foster caregiver. This meeting gives

the rescue organization personnel a chance to interview you and allows them to verify that the information that you submitted on your application was true and correct. Rescue volunteers make the Pug their first priority and may seem to be somewhat inquisitive. The information gathered from these meetings will then be used to create a profile of the suitable Pug for your family situation. It is at this time that an applicant may be considered preapproved for adoption.

References: Many Pug rescue organizations ask would-be Pug owners for references such as a veterinarian, kennel owner, or pet groomer. These professionals are asked to provide certain information on the care given to previous pets, as well as to verify information concerning additional pets listed on the application. In the absence of such references, a neighbor or other individual may be contacted to help establish an overall blueprint of the applicant's household.

Meeting the Pug

Once a Pug becomes available that fits a specific profile, the prospective family will be called to meet the Pug. This meeting may take place at the foster caregiver's home or the adopting family's home. Each member of the family will be asked to be present, and quite often any other dog in the household will be required to attend as well. The foster provider will then evaluate the interaction between the family and the Pug, as well as the interaction between the family's other dog and the new Pug. If all goes well, and the Pug seems at ease, the adoption will be authorized.

The Contract

The adoptive family will be asked to fill out and sign an adoption contract, which clearly states what is expected of the new home. These contracts are a legal agreement, so read carefully before you sign! Once again, each rescue organization has its own adoption contract. Follow-up phone calls and perhaps an unannounced visit will be conducted within a short period of time following the adoption. Nearly all rescue organizations make it mandatory to return the Pug to them for any reason, should the adoption not go as smoothly as hoped. Don't be afraid to call with questions and problems. Their goal is to see that every Pug that is placed by them remains in a safe, loving home!

Adoption

Adoption through a Pug rescue group is very rewarding. While the number of Pugs seeking new homes is on the rise, most rescue groups have a larger number of pre-approved applicants than there are Pugs available for adoption. Once an application has been submitted and approved, there are a number of factors affecting how long the wait will be to actually bring a Pug home. Those people who have expressed an interest in adopting a special needs Pug may have a better opportunity to adopt a Pug. Those applicants that have limited themselves to Pugs of specific ages, colors, or sex preferences may find the wait time extremely long. Flexibility can be the one factor that increases the chance to adopt a Pug. Waiting to adopt a Pug can be the ultimate test of patience.

Adoption Through Shelters/Humane Societies

The number of Pugs ending up in shelters has slowly decreased thanks to the formation of breed rescue groups and their ability to give home care to the many Pugs available for adoption. Many shelters are very willing to accept breed-specific applications, but some take a hit or miss approach by asking you to make weekly visits, just to check if a Pug has ended up needing adoption. Adopting a Pug from a humane organization begins with an application, which is then reviewed by a counselor. Shelters that are well run will ask specific questions and may deny the adoption if the shelter's policies are not met, or the Pug is not a suitable choice. In general, there are no home visits, or reference checks. Most Pugs that wind up in shelter facilities are strays and there is no history available on their background. While most shelters perform temperament testing and create a "Pug Profile," these Pugs do not have the benefit of being fostered in a home situation, and therefore may have hidden underlying issues that cannot be detected during the shelter's testing process. Many humane societies keep a listing of breed rescue organizations and may refer prospective Pug owners to those groups in their area. The shelter may also keep a list of names and numbers on file, in the hopes that a Pug will become available. While exploring all avenues of Pug adoption increases your chances of actually becoming a "Pug parent," the time spent waiting to adopt a Pug through a local shelter may actually be greater than the time spent waiting to adopt from a rescue group.

Retired Pugs

Another suggestion for adding an adult Pug to your family is to purchase a retired show dog or former breeding Pug from a reputable

show or hobby breeder. Breeders are too often incorrectly thought of as only a source for puppies; however, many have well-adjusted, house-trained adult Pugs seeking "life as a couch Pug-tato" after their show and breeding careers have ended. These Pugs are generally placed, at a reduced price, with families who will lavish them with the attention they so richly deserve, and quite frankly expect, in their retirement years.

The Joys of Adulthood

Middle-aged and older Pugs that find themselves in a new home are very often perfect angels. Given the chance, they will amuse their new families with antics that only a Pug with previous life experience can dream up. Young adult Pugs often misbehave slightly in their new homes in an attempt to establish their position within the new family environment. Many Pugs from one year of age to four years of age have unbridled energy and this stage is sometimes referred to as the "teen-age years."

It is this age group, these "teen-agers," that represent perhaps the largest number of Pugs relinquished to rescue groups and shelters. The use of a crate will keep these young-sters out of trouble when the new owner is unable to properly super-vise them. When adopting a Pug within this age group, setting up a schedule that can be strictly adhered to, one that has little variation in feeding times, potty breaks, owner departures and/or arrivals, helps to minimize the frustrations associated with adopting a secondhand Pug.

The reality is that most second-hand young- to middle-age Pugs have one or more behavioral issues that the previous owner was unable to correct or live with. Within the first 3 to 6 weeks, a re-homed Pug will exhibit any behavioral problems that may have existed in the past. For the Pug to succeed in the second home, the new owner must identify any problems quickly and formulate a workable treatment plan. Many Pug owners make excuses for their new Pug, especially regarding housetrain-ing issues, and try to live with the problem themselves. This treatment plan should include working with a qualified behaviorist or a trainer who specializes in positive reinforcement. Working on any behavioral problems with a positive approach is the best way to get the relationship between you and your new Pug off on the right foot. A consultation with your veterinarian may be beneficial, as medical causes for the behavioral problems should be ruledout.

Problems can occur with any rescued Pug, no matter what the age or sex. It is important to remember that the past may have been imperfect and sometimes painful, as in those Pugs who have suffered neglect or abuse. By structuring a positive future for your rescue Pug, behavioral issues can be overcome, creating the perfect Pug companion.

Separation Anxiety

Adult Pugs, particularly those that have been in multiple homes, may suddenly exhibit destructive behavior occurring only in the owner's absence. In these cases, this behavior is actually separation anxiety and is often accompanied by barking or whining, salivation, and urination or defecation. These Pugs are not angry because the owner has departed, but truly frantic when left alone. Separation anxiety causes a metabolic increase in heart rate and respiration, and induces a "panic attack" of sorts that cannot be controlled by the poor Pug. Crating or confinement may actually escalate the anxiety that may, in turn, cause the Pug to suffer injuries as he frantically tries to escape the confinement. Your veterinarian can help diagnose separation anxiety and offer treatment options and behavioral modification plans to ease the panic of these Pugs.

Chapter Six
The Pug's Palate

It is no secret that to a Pug food represents the center of the universe, and the prospect of that day's meal is a reason to get up and greet each new day. Most Pugs will eat just about anything that is put in front of them, including some things that may not be a part of the normal canine diet. The saying "You are what you eat" is actually very close to the truth when it comes to the nutritional makeup of your Pug's diet. Feeding your Pug a well-balanced, high-quality diet that is appropriate for his age and activity level is important to his overall condition, health, and longevity. Choosing your Pug's diet is the single most important decision you will make that can directly impact your Pug's long-term health.

Labels

In order to make an informed decision regarding which food is best for your Pug, you need to understand how various types of dog foods are prepared. By learning to read the labels on pet foods, you can begin to understand the basic ingredients that are included in each bag or can of dog food and the spe-

cific roles that they play in maintaining the overall health and condition of a Pug. Quality ingredients, in the recommended dietary proportions, are the keys to finding a balanced Pug-appropriate diet.

The label on every commercially prepared diet provides information on the nutritional value of the package contents. Each label must contain values on four important nutrients: crude protein, crude fiber, crude fat, and moisture. These values are referred to as the Guaranteed Analysis. Crude protein and crude fat are expressed as a minimum guarantee (% Min.), which indicates the least amount of the specific nutrient, which must be present in the formula. Fiber and moisture are expressed as a maximum guarantee (% Max.), which reflects the largest amount of the specific nutrient present in the formula. When analyzing the Guaranteed Analysis it is important to remember that the percentage may actually be much higher or lower than indicated, as these percentages are considered maximums and minimums.

The ingredient panel defines the specific makeup of the food. The ingredients are listed in descending order, with the largest quantity listed first. Most dog food labels also contain feeding instructions or guidelines. These amounts are recommendations. Quite often the actual amount you will need to feed to achieve the proper weight and coat health for your Pug may be less than the label suggests, although your Pug may try to tell you differently. Variables such as your Pug's activity level, health status, and even the local climate may also play a significant role in the amount of food that your Pug needs to maintain optimum body condition.

Note: When purchasing your Pug's food, be sure to check the label for the expiration date or product freshness date. Dog food that has been stored for a lengthy period of time may lose some of the vital nutrients and should be avoided.

Nutrients

While analyzing the food label provides information on the quantity and type of ingredients, it is the quality of the specific ingredients that ultimately determines the usability of the product and the health benefits to your Pug. In order to evaluate the quality of ingredients, you must understand the basic nutrients that make up your Pug's food, and their role in overall nutrition.

Proteins: Proteins are perhaps the most important nutrients for the overall health and condition of your Pug. Protein has a variety of functions in the Pug body, most notably the supplying of amino acids. These amino acids are the building blocks for the musculoskeletal system—muscles, ligaments, cartilage, and tendons. Amino acids also play a role in the formation of hair and nails. Proteins are also a major component of proper hormone production and play a key role in the body's ability to produce disease-fighting antibodies.

The proteins in dog foods can be animal-based, plant-based, or a combination of both types. Animal-based proteins such as chicken, beef, fish, and lamb provide all the essential amino acids needed for healthy development. Animal-based proteins are more easily digestible than plant-based proteins, which may lack some essential amino acids.

Carbohydrates: Carbohydrates are the nutrients that are primarily responsible for the body's energy reserves. Nearly all carbohydrates are derived from plant proteins, but some carbohydrate sources are more digestible than others. By utilizing combinations of carbohydrates, dog food manufacturers have been able to manipulate such important metabolic functions as blood glucose levels. Not all carbohydrate sources are easy for the Pug to digest. Foods that utilize such carbohydrates as cornmeal, barley, and wheat in their formulas are more digestible and provide a better source of energy.

Fats: Fats are the nutrients that play a significant role in several physical characteristics of every Pug. The fat content of dog food is often the factor that determines palatability, with foods containing increased amounts of fat often preferred. The percentage of fat also impacts the overall weight of your Pug, as a high number of calories are derived from fat. Dietary fats also determine the health status of a Pug's coat. Pugs that are fed a diet containing decreased amounts of fat often have coats that are dry and brittle, and skin that is flaky.

Fiber: Fiber quality and quantity varies significantly among different brands of dog food. Fiber plays a role in digestibility, with moderately fermentable fiber benefiting the health of the intestinal tract. Some weight reduction diets utilize high levels of poorly fermentable fiber, which increases stool volume and offers no significant nutritional value. Diets with an increased amount of

❖ PUG POINT ❖

Carnivores

While all dogs are considered omnivores, eating both animal and plant material, their body structure is designed to be fed more as a carnivore. The gastrointestinal tract is not equipped to digest large amounts of plant proteins. Pugs thrive on a diet with more animal-based protein than plant.

fiber or a diet that contains poorly digestible fiber also contribute to increased gas production, something most owners would rather their Pugs do without.

The Great Grain Controversy

A great deal of attention and marketing by dog food companies has recently centered on "grain-free" diets. This has led to a misconception or myth that has been populated on the Internet that all grains in dog food are bad, or that grain-free diets are somehow healthier for dogs. Grains are the main source for carbohydrates, which provide energy.

The reality is that the type and quality of grain used in the diet is important. The most common grains in commercial dog food are corn and wheat. Just as humans can sometimes be sensitive or intolerant to some grains (think of all the gluten-free foods you now see advertised), individual

Pugs may need a food with a different grain, or one that is grain-free.

Symptoms of grain intolerance may include scratching at the ears, licking of the paws, and licking of the rear end. If you suspect your Pug may have sensitivity to grains in his diet, please consult your veterinarian.

Special ingredients: The evolution of improvements in the overall quality of dog food has brought about an increase in the use of ingredients that can be added for special purposes.

Fatty acid supplements are added to many dog foods to contribute to better skin and coat health. Fatty acids also play an important role in the body's inflammatory response. The most commonly mentioned fatty acids are Omega-3 and Omega-6 fatty acids. Omega-3 fatty acids are often found in fishmeal or oil, flax, and canola. Omega-6 fatty acids are found in chicken fat and corn. Fatty acids are essential for a Pug to maintain a healthy skin and coat. An important piece in the fatty acid puzzle is including both Omega-3 and Omega-6 fatty acids in your Pug's diet. These important nutrients must be in a properly balanced ratio to increase your Pug's inflammatory response (Omega-3 and Omega-6 fatty acids are a natural antiinflammatory), and provide optimum coat and skin condition. Premium dog foods target a ratio of Omega-6 that is five to six times higher than Omega-3 fatty acids.

Senior Pugs, or those Pugs with arthritis or other orthopedic diseases, may benefit from a diet that contains the addition of nutraceuticals for improving joint health. Many high-quality dog foods now contain such ingredients as glucosamine, chondroitin, and MSM to aid in the Pug's own production of healthy joint fluid. There is some discussion among veterinarians and breeders as to whether the usable amounts of these ingredients in such diets are actually high enough to render much benefit. More research is most likely needed to definitively answer this question, but many Pug owners do report that their Pug has improved mobility after eating these diets for several weeks.

The new wave of dog food additives refer to ingredients that inhibit tartar buildup and help in overall dental health. These additives may be present in the form of microcrystals that temporarily bond to the teeth and limit the amount of bacterial growth, which is the catalyst of plaque formation. Other dental control measures that dog food companies are using include changing the size, shape, or texture of the dry food to create an increase in the abrasive action on the teeth while chewing.

Diet Types

Over the last 20 years, the pet food market and dog foods in particular, have become the most competitive retail industry, offering the Pug owner an endless variety of choices. More recently, the appearance of unique types and textures of foods create a difficult decision for Pug owners who are attempting to select the most beneficial diet for their Pug's health. Selecting a diet is not easy and requires a bit of research by the Pug owner to make an informed decision.

To begin your search for the perfect food, you should decide whether you want to feed a commercially prepared diet or a freshly prepared alternative. Commercial diets offer the option of a variety of choices, all prepared to greatly improve the health and longevity of your Pug. Commercially prepared diets offer choices with a selection of meat-based options and are available in bite-sized pieces to better suit a Pug's unique dental structure. There is even a diet produced and marketed specifically for the unique needs of the Pug! This food offers a unique shape to promote healthy Pug teeth, L-carnitine for maintaining healthy weight, fatty acids for healthy skin and wrinkles, and glucosamine and chondroitin for healthy joints. Commercial dog food diets are readily available, with "premium" diets consisting of better-quality, highly digestible ingredients, marketed in pet stores, veterinary hospitals, and dog food "superstore" retailers.

Commercially prepared diets themselves offer the Pug owner several different feeding options:

• Dry foods contain less than 20 percent moisture, and while the texture provides some tartar control, dry food alone is often the one commercially prepared food that some Pugs will refuse to eat.

• Semi-moist diets are made up of between 20 percent moisture and 64 percent moisture and quickly become a Pug's favorite diet due in part to their texture. Semi-moist diets may contain proportionately higher amounts of sugars, making them more palatable than dry foods. These

sugars are used as preservatives, as well as a component in creating the unique shapes of semimoist diets.

• Commercially prepared canned foods contain at least 65 percent moisture and are often the "filet mignon" of a Pug's diet. Canned diets are available in nearly every animal-based flavor, as well as offering the Pug choices including vegetables, grains, and various shapes and textures. Selecting a canned food can be a mind-numbing experience for the Pug owner. A word of advice: Most Pugs enjoy a wide variety of canned flavor options.

Note: Keep in mind that neither semi-moist diets nor canned foods offer the cleansing action in the mouth that dry foods can, and a diet consisting strictly of canned food or semi-moist morsels may actually contribute to an increase in the severity or incidence of dental problems in the Pug.

Additional Diet Types

Two additional types of commercially prepared diets have recently become available, though neither diet is considered to be new.

• Frozen diets are available in some areas of the United States and Canada. These diets, when thawed properly, become extremely palatable and are considered a fresher alternative to commercially prepared dry dog foods. Not all Pug owners have access to these diets, however, and storing frozen dog food may not be a practical option for some. The high cost of frozen diets may also deter a dog owner from using this feeding option as a primary diet.

• Dog food rolls are now being sold in the same stores that carry other premium diets. These rolls are preserved naturally and must be refrigerated once opened, or frozen for long-term storage. Most Pugs find dog food rolls to be particularly tasty, but the cost may make them too expensive to be fed as a primary diet. Dog food roll diets are a fresher alternative to canned and can be added to increase the acceptance of a commercially prepared dry dog food.

Recommendations

Most veterinarians and Pug breeders universally recommend feeding a commercially prepared dry food, supplemented by a small amount of canned food added to the dry portion. By mixing the dry food with a small amount of warm water, you can also increase the moisture, making the plain, boring dry food more acceptable to nearly every Pug.

Alternatives

With recent trends toward healthier eating and natural diets in our own lives, Pug owners may look for better, fresher alternatives to commercially prepared diets, which more closely complement their own lifestyles. There are two types of freshly prepared diets, which are gaining popularity with Pug owners:

Home-cooked diets may be prepared by the Pug owner to offer a fresh food that contains a smor-

---

❖ PUG POINT ❖

Overfeeding

More is not always better. Overfeeding can result in joint and leg problems affecting both the forelimbs and hind limbs of Pug puppies. Too much of certain vitamins and minerals, such as calcium and phosphorous, has also been proven to increase the incidence of hip dysplasia, hyperparathyroidism, and other bone diseases. There is a recent trend among some Pug breeders to change puppies from a diet formulated for growth to one that is formulated for adult maintenance at or around four months of age. This is based on research in larger breed dogs that suggests that orthopedic problems such as hip dysplasia are, in part, influenced by diet at an early age.

The decision to transition your Pug from a diet formulated for puppies to one that is formulated for adults should be discussed with your veterinarian.

---

gasbord of ingredients, and a Pug quickly learns to expect no less! Veterinarians can offer home-cooked diet recipes that are designed to meet the nutritional needs of Pugs with very specific medical problems or conditions.

BARF: In addition to home-cooked diets, there are an increasing number of breeders and veterinarians who feed natural raw diets or

BARF diets. (BARF stands for Bones and Raw Food). BARF diets are based on the belief that dogs have thrived on raw diets for centuries before the invention of commercially prepared dog foods, and proponents of BARF diets also believe that raw food diets offer countless health benefits, such as helping to boost the digestive and immune systems.

Risks

If you choose to feed either a home-cooked diet or BARF diet to your Pug, there are several very important facts to remember. The first issue is to find out whether the diet has been thoroughly tested to meet the mandatory nutritional requirements set forth by the Association of American Feed Control Officials. Unfortunately, very few BARF diets or home-cooked diets have been through any feeding trials or laboratory testing procedures, but are prepared, marketed, and fed anyway. Secondly, it is important to be sure that the diet contains all of the basic required vitamins and minerals. While these diets are prepared with a variety of fresh ingredients, many need to be fed with a vitamin and mineral supplement in order to meet the Pug's basic requirements. Finally, the preparation of both of these diets plays a key role in keeping your Pug healthy. When purchasing the ingredients that are to be used to makeup these diets, the Pug owner should make every effort to buy high-quality, fresh beef, poultry, and other meat products.

Raw meats bring with them a higher risk of bacterial contamination such as salmonella, *E. coli,* and listeria if not stored and prepared properly. In addition, your Pug's food bowl should be properly washed and disinfected daily to avoid any potential health risks to both you and your Pug. Parasitic infections may also be a risk for Pugs that are fed raw diets. BARF diets may be prepared with larger breeds of dogs in mind, and Pugs that are fed these diets, many containing bones or bone chips, may also be at a greater risk of intestinal obstruction or perforation if the diet is poorly prepared.

Understanding the risks involved with home-cooked and raw diets is an important part of making the decision regarding your Pug's nutritional health. Home-cooked diets and raw diets (fresh or frozen) are significantly more expensive than commercially prepared dog foods, and the potential health benefits may be outweighed by the costs and risks involved.

Life-Stage or Activity-Based Diets

Whether you have chosen to feed your Pug a commercially prepared diet, fresh, or frozen food, or a combination of both, the job of figuring out your Pug's specific needs, and the food that best fits that stage now begins. Diets are often prepared for a very specific stage in a Pug's life, or for an appropriate activity level.

If your Pug is less than one year old, the diet you choose to feed should be formulated for growth. You may also choose to feed a diet that has been even more specifically formulated for small or toy breeds, those formulated for a breed with an adult weight reaching no more than 20 pounds (9 kg). Diets that are formulated for puppies should meet the minimum nutritional requirements that include an increased energy content to meet the higher energy requirements of an active toy breed puppy. The ingredients used should be quality ingredients, not fillers or predominately vegetable-based proteins. If you choose to feed a premium dog food, it is not necessary, nor recommended, to supplement the diet with vitamins or minerals. The ratios of vitamins and minerals in these diets have been scientifically formulated to ensure the health of your growing Pug.

The feeding guidelines for Pug puppies are equally important. Pug puppies should be portion fed, or given a specific, measured amount of food that is offered several times daily based on the puppy's age. Toy breed puppies are prone to swings in metabolic blood glucose levels. Offering frequent, small meals throughout the day can control these levels. In addition, Pugs that are portion fed are less likely to become overweight, as the owners are closely monitoring and controlling the amount of food consumed each day, not the food-obsessed Pug. Pug puppies under six months old should be fed no less than three times daily, while Pugs between six

months and one year old should be fed twice a day. Fresh water should be available at all times during the day for every Pug puppy.

For the average Pug over one year of age, a diet that meets the nutritional maintenance needs of adult dogs should be chosen. The average adult Pug requires a diet that contains moderate protein levels and lower levels of fat to reduce the chance of unhealthy weight gain. The essential fatty acids must be present, however, to ensure a healthy Pug coat and minimize shedding. Once again, the owner must control the daily portion, as Pugs will gladly consume a great deal more than the minimum amount of their basic nutritional and caloric requirements when the portion control is left up to them. Keep in mind that the feed-

Assessing Body Condition and Obesity

The following table is the universal assessment of body condition and obesity:

Thin—Ribs easy to palpate, tops of vertebrae visible, obvious waist

Ideal—Ribs palpable with no excess fat covering, waist observed behind ribs

Heavy—Ribs palpable with some difficulty, waist absent, fat pads (deposits) visible just above hips

Obese—Ribs not palpable, large fat pads visible, waist absent, abdominal fat present

ing guidelines found on commercially prepared dog foods may be quite a bit more than your Pug really needs to maintain optimum body condition. These guidelines are recommendations that may need to be cut by as much as half if weight control becomes a problem and your Pug's meals are going "straight from the lips to the hips."

Active, highly energetic adult Pugs may actually require an increase in the amount of calories that they consume on a daily basis. Performance diets, high in nutrient-dense energy, should be fed to your Pug if he is competing in a performance event, active in obedience or agility classes, or just seems to have trouble maintaining adequate body weight.

The Obese Pug

The most common nutritionally based health problem facing the Pug, and the most common overall health problem today, is the astronomical number of overweight and outright obese Pugs. We all know that the Pug's job, its purpose, is to be a couch potato or a bed hog. This activity-challenged status plays an important role in the "packing on" of excess pounds. Poor body condition, in the form of excess weight, is the number one cause of cardiovascular disease, diabetes, and nonhereditary ortho-pedic problems, such as torn cruci-ate ligaments, spinal disc problems, and knee problems, facing the Pug today.

The normal metabolism of a Pug decreases slightly around one year of age to eighteen months of age. In order to avoid "putting on the pounds," the caloric intake must also decrease at this time if the energy level or activity level decreases. The breed standard for the Pug gives an ideal weight of 14 to 18 pounds (6–8 kg); however, many Pugs today have an optimum body weight of 18 to 20 pounds (8–9.1 kg). For many Pugs, especially the ladies, a body weight of 22 pounds (10 kg) or more sig-nals that there is a significant weight problem.

To determine your Pug's "body score," look at your Pug's shape directly above him. The body shape that you are looking for is an hour-glass, with the hips and shoulders approximately the same width, and a small indentation at the waistline. Placing your hands on your Pug's sides, you should be able to feel the ribs with a slight covering of flesh over them. If you have to really poke with your fingers to find the ribs, or the overhead view of your Pug's body shape is more of a rectangle or oval, your Pug is carrying excess weight.

Correcting the Problem

Obesity is a potentially life-threat-ening nutritional problem that can be corrected by you, the owner. Choosing a diet that contains no

more than 18 percent protein and a maximum of 9 percent fat will sig-nificantly lower your Pug's caloric intake. It is also important to monitor the types of treats and the quan-tity of snacks that you give your Pug each day. All too often there is one family member who, on a daily basis, indulges her Pug with a car-nival of treats while she herself is eating. Vegetables such as baby carrots may be substituted for cook-ies. If your Pug is obese and you are not measuring the exact amount of food that he receives each day, this now becomes mandatory. Use a standard measuring cup to measure the amount you have been previ-ously feeding and you might be sur-prised at the actual quantity of food you have been giving your glutton-ous Pug.

As a guideline, the average adult Pug, fed a quality, dry, commer-cially prepared diet, does not usually require more than a measured cup of food per day to meet his caloric energy requirements. Any Pug that is offered more than the minimum volume of food that is necessary to

Exercise

As is true for any weight-loss program, the weight reduction goal cannot be achieved without an increase in metabolism. Increasing your overweight Pug's daily exercise is mandatory if you want to achieve any noticeable weight loss. A brisk walk around the block twice a day may be enough to initiate the increase in metabolism. As your Pug's exercise tolerance increases, increase the length of the walk or speed up the pace a bit, to continue to ensure adequate weight loss.

Changing Eating Habits Through Veterinary Science

If your Pug is truly obese and his quality of life is severely impacted by his own gluttony, newly introduced veterinary diets that actually alter your Pug's metabolism to more closely resemble that of a lean Pug are now available. These diets do work quite well to help your Pug shed unwanted pounds easily, but they are only available by prescription through your veterinarian and may have to be continued indefinitely to help keep those pesky pounds off.

A prescription "diet aid" in a liquid form has also been introduced that curbs your Pug's appetite. When given daily, this medication decreases your Pug's overwhelming desire to eat, making it much more difficult for you to overfeed. Weight loss is achieved by a decrease in caloric intake combined with an increase in exercise or activity.

maintain optimum body condition will eagerly eat the excess, beg for more, and quickly become obese.

After assessing the amount of food you are feeding, you may find it necessary to decrease the amount of food to a more reasonable, Pug-sized ration. Don't be surprised if your Pug gives an award-winning performance as a starving orphan after the sudden decrease in volume. A slight adjustment in feeding schedules may help to overcome the "starving Pug" syndrome. By splitting the total amount that you feed into smaller, multiple meals offered at several times each day, the Pug's stomach always contains food. This presence of food helps to convince your Pug that the stomach is not quite as empty, and food in the stomach equals a very happy Pug.

These options should only be considered after discussing your Pug's weight with your veterinarian.

The Finicky Eater

This is a rather short topic, as a "finicky Pug" is usually unheard of. When a previously ravenous Pug refuses to eat, it usually means that he is not feeling well. If you are concerned, seek your veterinarian's advice.

Many well-intentioned owners who baby their Pugs (and let's face it, who can resist babying them just a little?) may soon create a poor mealtime eater. Most Pugs will eat as much and as often as the owner will indulge them. They quickly learn, and at a very early age, whether their owner is a pushover when it comes to feeding time. A Pug that has a bowl of food available at all times soon learns that he doesn't need to consume a large amount at any one time. The bowl is always waiting there, filled with food, whenever he gets bored, tired, or simply feels the need to snack. This may create a Pug that is disinterested in eating his meals.

In general, Pugs thrive on a diet that is consistent and routine, rather than constantly changing. It is important for Pug owners to choose a quality diet and remain firm in feeding that diet to their Pug. Switching diets when you think that your Pug may be bored with the current diet, or adding tasty tidbits to entice your Pug to eat, teaches him to hold out on eating to see if you are going to offer something better. Let's face it—Pugs live for food and there aren't too many Pugs that are going to refuse to eat for more than a day or two once they realize that you are serious about mealtime choices and rations.

If you are one of those owners who must offer a variety of flavors to please your Pug's palate, try to add canned foods containing various flavors, ingredients, and textures, rather than adding table scraps. Make sure that the food is well mixed to avoid a "picky Pug" that chooses to eat only the meaty morsels. You can also try to spice up the food by adding finely chopped bits of roll diets to your Pug's normal meal. By utilizing the various forms of nutritionally complete diets in combination, you can be sure that the nutritional well-being of your Pug is being met.

To sum up: Preventing your Pug from becoming a poor eater and ensuring that your Pug maintains proper body condition is easily accomplished if the young Pug is fed on a strict schedule, offered a consistent, balanced diet, and between-meal snacks are kept to a minimum.

Chapter Seven

The Pretty Pug

The Pug is considered to be a low-maintenance dog when it comes to keeping him clean and well groomed. This is generally true, but there are several beauty routines that need to be performed on a regular basis to keep your Pug looking, feeling, and smelling his best. Routine grooming is also an excellent way to discover medical problems or concerns early, so prompt treatment can be given.

Coat Types

Many Pug owners are unaware that there are two coat types or lengths of hair in Pugs that may affect the way in which the owner approaches the overall grooming.

The Single Coat

Pugs that have a single coat appear to be sleeker, as the individual hairs lay closely on top of each other in a very close fit. The single coat is more characteristic of the older-style, or Victorian-type Pug. The single-coated Pug will shed the close-fitting guard hairs year-round, though the volume of hair that the owner must vacuum is significantly less than a Pug with a double coat. The single coat is the predominant coat type in most bloodlines that contain a large number of black Pugs in the background, and of the black Pug in general.

The Double Coat

The double coat has appeared to become the more common coat type in Pugs, especially in fawn bloodlines. The Pug with a double coat actually has a plush, thick undercoat covered by the dense guard hairs that make up the single coat. The undercoat in double-coated Pugs gives the illusion of a much softer appearance, almost a fuzzy bear resemblance in young Pug puppies. The double-coated Pug requires lengthier brushing to remove the excess hair and to maintain a healthy coat. The double-coated Pug sheds considerably more than the single coat, as the dense undercoat is lost twice yearly, in addition to the constant replacing of the guard hairs. Female Pugs, particularly those that have not been spayed, seem to shed more and for a longer period of time than the male Pugs.

While there are many attributes of the Pug that make the breed appealing, the constant shedding is not one of them. The loose hair and dander that accompany it make the Pug a poor choice for families with allergies.

Bathing Your Pug

The description "low maintenance" gives the impression that routine bathing is relatively unnecessary for a Pug. This statement is generally true of the Pug, which typically requires a bath only every three or four months. There are always exceptions to this rule, particularly if your Pug finds mud puddles to be better than a swimming pool, or Mother Nature doesn't cooperate during the wet spring and fall months. Any Pug whose coat is dirty runs the increased risk of bacterial infections of the skin and should be

bathed to be kept feeling clean and healthy.

Shampoo

Choosing the right shampoo can be difficult, but has a significant impact on the look and feel of your Pug's coat. A dog's hair coat has a different pH than human hair. Routine bathing should always be done with a shampoo formulated for dogs. Human shampoos can be very drying, damaging the beautiful Pug coat. For the Pug that has a healthy coat and no skin problems, the choice should be a general deodorizing shampoo or puppy shampoo. Oatmeal-based shampoos often contain extra emollients to help maintain the coat's soft look and feel, while decreasing any itchiness your Pug may occasionally feel. Oatmeal shampoos are an excellent choice for routine bathing.

Color-specific shampoos are also available for both black and fawn coats and produce a vibrant coat color. These shampoos may be used for routine bathing as long as they are not used too frequently. Color-enhancing shampoos can be more drying or stripping than deodorizing shampoos. Following a bath using a color-specific shampoo, you might want to add a light coat conditioner to replace any lost moisture.

Flea and tick shampoos: Shampoos are also available for external parasite control, specifically fleas and ticks. If you suspect that your Pug may have a flea problem or you have removed a tick or two from the coat, it is a good idea to bathe him with a flea and tick shampoo. Flea and tick shampoos may have conditioning agents added to them to replace moisture lost during the bath. They may be very damaging to the coat if used for routine bathing.

Skin problems: It should be mentioned that a variety of shampoos are marketed for skin problems. Many are available at pet stores, while others are sold only through your veterinarian. Shampoos that are aimed at specific skin or coat conditions can be used safely and effectively if the owner has already received a diagnosis of the condition from her veterinarian, and that the correct shampoo is being used as directed for the condition. These medicated shampoos include antibacterial shampoos, antifungal shampoos, shampoos that contain antihistamines to control itching, and others that combine medications.

Shed-Less shampoos and treatments: There are some new shampoos and treatments that are specially formulated to loosen dead hair, revitalize new hair growth, and—with regular use—decrease shedding. These shampoos and treatments are probably most effective when your Pug regularly visits a professional groomer, as they have the bathing equipment and expertise to keep your Pug's coat looking its best.

Bathing Techniques

Bathing a Pug can be a simple task if your Pug is cooperative and

enjoys the attention, or it can resemble a wrestling match with a grizzly bear if he feels clean enough already. There are a few simple steps that should be done routinely prior to bathing your Pug to prevent medical problems from occurring after the bath.

Ears: Many Pugs have ears that are very sensitive to slight increases of moisture in the ear canal. To prevent excess moisture from entering the ear canal, place a cotton ball gently into each ear canal prior to the start of the bath. Once you have finished bathing your Pug, remove the cotton balls. If the cotton is soaked with water, you may want to clean the ears with an ear-cleaning solution to help dry up the ear canal.

Eyes: The Pug's eyes are very vulnerable to injury during the bathing process. Care should be taken to lower the risk of injury or irritation during the bath, particularly when using a medicated shampoo or flea and tick product. A drop or two of mineral oil, carefully placed in each eye before bathing, coats the sensitive cornea and protects it from chemical irritation and burns. Artificial tear ointments may also be used in the eye if you do not have mineral oil; however, these solutions do not offer the complete coverage of mineral oil and may not remain a protective barrier for the same length of time.

The correct bathing procedure is as follows:

1. Medicate eyes and place cotton balls in ears.

2. Completely wet your Pug's coat with lukewarm water, beginning with the neck, spine, and tail and working your way down the body and legs. Gently spray the earflaps and forehead, but avoid spraying water directly into your Pug's face and ears. Remember, double-coated Pugs have thicker coats and the water must completely soak both the undercoat and guard hairs.

3. Apply the shampoo to your Pug's neck and spine. Use your fingers to work the shampoo into a nice lather that can be massaged into the body and down the legs. Pour a small amount of shampoo into your palms, rub your hands together, and apply this to the outside of the earflaps if needed. This can be repeated for the application of additional shampoo to the legs and underbelly. Allow the lather to remain on your Pug as directed by your shampoo label.

4. Rinse your Pug completely, beginning with the neck. Move the water down the spine to the tail, and then down each side until no lather remains. Gently rinse the earflaps. Don't forget to rinse your Pug's tummy and between the front and rear legs. If your Pug wants to shake off the excess water, holding the skin on the neck just below the ear works to keep you from getting a bath too.

5. Dry your Pug with a soft, fluffy bath towel.

Here are some important steps to remember about giving your Pug a bath.

• Once you begin to bathe your Pug, follow the specific directions given on the shampoo that you have

chosen. For medicated or flea and tick shampoos, you must follow the guidelines suggested to produce the desired effect.

• Pay particular attention to any soap residue that may remain in the coat, especially if your Pug is double coated. Excess soap that remains on the skin or trapped in the undercoat often causes skin irritation, resulting in a Pug that continually chews or scratches, which, in turn, leads to further skin and coat problems.

Drying: Drying your Pug can be quicker if you do it in several steps. While your Pug is still in the bathtub, use your fingers to squeeze the excess water from the coat. Your hands can become a substitute squeegee, pulling moisture from the neck and spine, down the body area toward the legs, and off your shivering Pug. This hands-on approach also allows you to double-check for any shampoo that may have been missed during the rinsing process. Towel drying is very important once the excess water has been removed, in order to speed up the drying process. Drying your Pug with a pet or car chamois can be an excellent first step prior to towel drying. The Pug's thick coat often retains water and without adequate towel drying, may take up to several hours to dry completely.

Many owners find that using a hair dryer or commercial pet dryer helps to loosen much of the remaining dead hair following a bath. Using a dryer is often a two-person job however, as many Pugs do not like the sound of

the dryer or the air blowing at them, especially near their sensitive eyes and ears. You can make this task more pleasant by offering your Pug small bites of tasty treats during the drying process.

Having a sense of humor helps when deciding to bathe and dry your Pug at home. If wrestling and wrangling your Pug in the tub is not your idea of a fun afternoon, you can always employ the services of a professional groomer!

Brushing Your Pug

The routine grooming of the Pug should include a quick brushing or combing at least once a week. This easy grooming step removes the dead hair that has not yet made it onto your furniture and clothing. A weekly brushing helps to stimulate the hair follicles to produce new hair and increases the distribution of essential oils throughout the coat. Routine weekly brushing also allows you to check for any health problems such as external parasites, skin irritations, and tumors. Most Pugs enjoy the physical attention of each brushing and will sit patiently waiting for the owner to finish what they consider to be a total body massage. During the peak periods of shedding, a quick daily brushing will help to drastically reduce the amount of hair your Pug deposits in its environment. Some owners will actually vacuum their Pug during these increased shedding months.

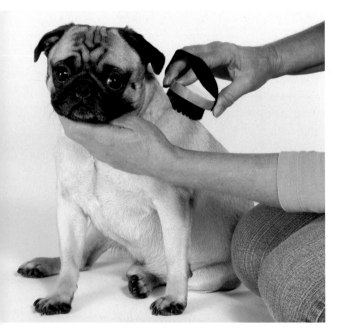

Grooming Tools

The right grooming tool for your Pug's hair coat can make an enormous difference in how much hair you collect from your Pug's coat. There are several choices available, and each one can be appropriate for brushing your Pug.

1. The bristle brush is perhaps the most commonly used brush. A quality bristle brush has tightly packed, short bristles, which stimulate and distribute the hair's own oils, leaving the coat looking shiny and healthy. The bristle brush is excellent for removing dead outer coat or guard hairs, but is not designed to really get into the undercoat. The bristle brush is an excellent choice for grooming the Pug that is not shedding excessively.

2. The slicker brush is widely used to remove the undercoat and pull dead hair from the coat. Slicker brushes are flat in shape with metal bristles that can be closely packed together, referred to as fine, or widely spaced, known as coarse. Most Pug owners find that a medium to coarse brush works best, and that the bristle length should be relatively short.

Note: When using a slicker brush to remove undercoat, be careful not to put too much pressure on the brush during the brushing process. Slicker brushes can be quite irritating if used too harshly, and this "brush burn" can cause local skin irritations which your Pug may continue to aggravate by scratching or constant chewing. A slicker brush should be pulled through your Pug's undercoat in short, brisk, light strokes in order to remove the maximum amount of dead hair.

3. A metal comb can be an excellent additional grooming tool for the thicker areas of a Pug's body. A finely spaced comb easily removes hair from the neck, shoulder, thigh and hip areas where the coat tends to be thicker and sometimes difficult to completely strip of dead hair.

4. Perhaps the Pug's favorite choice for a grooming tool is the grooming glove or rubber grooming mitt. The grooming glove is slipped on over the owner's hand like a mitten and has small, rubber teeth or bumps on the palm portion instead of bristles. Brushing is made easy as you simply "pet" your Pug and the dead outer coat is quickly removed. Your Pug will thoroughly enjoy the additional quality time together, and even very active Pugs can be brushed after they fall asleep on the couch. The glove does not remove a lot of excessive undercoat, but the rubber bristles do offer a miniature skin massage for your pampered Pug.

5. De-shedding tools such as the Furminator® can be a great way to cut down on the dead hair and undercoat that all Pugs deposit on furniture and clothing. When used once or twice weekly, these tools remove dead coat and can significantly reduce shedding.

Ear Care

The Pug's ear can be an unfortunate source of trouble if not tended to on a regular basis. Ear infections are common because the folded ear produces an ear canal that is dark, warm, and damp—the perfect environment for bacterial growth. Routine grooming must also include cleaning your Pug's ears regularly, preferably on a weekly basis to inhibit both yeast and bacteria from taking over the ear canal.

Routine cleaning should begin with an appropriate ear-cleaning solution, which can be purchased from your veterinarian or pet supply store. Whenever it is possible, choose a product that leaves the ear canal with an acidic pH level. Bacterial growth is significantly slower in environments that have a lower pH. Rubbing alcohol is an acceptable alternative if you do not have another cleaning solution available.

Cleaning your Pug's ears is a relatively easy process, but may require two people—one to hold the squirming Pug and one to do the actual cleaning. To begin, choose an elevated location such as a tabletop. Placing your Pug off of the floor puts you in control and eliminates the "four feet on the floor" escape route. Lift your Pug's earflap up to expose the canal and squeeze three to four drops of the cleaning solution into the ear canal. While still holding the earflap up, use your opposite hand to gently massage the base of the ear canal. This loosens debris in the ear canal and helps the cleaning solution cut through any wax buildup.

Use a cotton ball that has several additional drops of the cleaning solution on it to wipe out the canal, removing any debris and excess fluid from the ear. Dry cotton should not be used to clean the ear canal as it can be very abrasive to the sensitive middle ear, especially if there are any signs of ulcers or infection. A cotton-tipped applicator that has been soaked with cleaning solution can be used to wipe out the many crevices and creases in the external canal.

A small amount of wax may be present in the ear canal each time that you clean your Pug's ears. Normal wax is light brown to yellow in color and relatively odorless. Any thick, dark, black debris, excessive amounts of wax, or an ear canal that has a strong, unpleasant odor are all signals that your Pug may have an ear problem. If you suspect any ear problems, contact your veterinarian for a thorough ear examination.

Pedicures

Giving your Pug a pedicure, also known as nail trimming, is the most difficult grooming task for most Pug owners. Nail trimming is never on a Pug's list of favorite pastimes; it will be tolerated by some, and despised by all others. Trimming your Pug's nails is quite often a two- or three-person job, and may need to be performed by your veterinarian or a professional dog groomer.

Most Pugs put up quite a fight whenever the nail trimmers are brought into view. Why do you need to routinely fight such a battle when your Pug so adamantly objects to it? Pugs use their front feet to wipe their faces, similar to the way a cat uses its front paws to wash itself. Maintaining short nails is extremely important to prevent self-inflicted, accidental eye injuries. The dewclaws, the small nails located on the inside of the front legs, should be trimmed as short as possible. These dewclaws may be absent if your Pug's breeder had them removed shortly after birth. If your Pug will tolerate nail trimming weekly or twice a month, you will need to remove only the very tip of each nail to keep the short length.

Trimmers

There are several types of nail trimmers available that can be used successfully to trim your Pug's nails. Guillotine-type trimmers use a blade that slices through the nail. They generally come in two sizes, with the small/medium size adequate for a Pug. These trimmers can be somewhat awkward to hold and may be difficult for some owners to use. Pliers-type trimmers are available in many handle sizes and various blade sizes. For many Pug owners, having the option of different handle types makes finding one that is comfortable to use a much easier task.

Technique

Whatever your preference is for a trimmer, begin to practice trimming by removing just the nail tip. Once you are comfortable with "tipping" the nail, you may then begin to try to trim the nails back a bit further toward the footpad. The nail has a vein located in the center of each toenail, and cutting too closely to the "quick" or end of the vein can result in some bleeding. There are styptic powders available that, when applied to the bleeding nail, quickly lessen and eventually stop the bleeding. It is a good idea to have one of these powders close by during each nail trim. The "quick" may be visible as a dark, pink shade in the center of light-colored toenails. This makes the visual identification of the quick much easier.

Some Pug owners choose to grind the nails down with a rotary grinding tool. It may be possible to grind the nails short with potentially less bleeding. Some Pugs tolerate having their nails ground down better than trimming them with a trimmer.

You may find that by pairing yummy food rewards with nail clipping, your Pug suddenly becomes much more tolerant of the entire process. Jars of meat baby food, string cheese, small bits of chicken breast, or peanut butter on a spoon are some examples of food rewards that may tempt your Pug to be a little more brave when the clippers come out.

Wrinkle Care

Care of the prominent nose wrinkle is just as important as routine ear care. Once again, the nasal fold is an excellent breeding ground for yeast and bacteria and should be cleaned regularly. Cleaning once a week will help to control any odor from the nasal fold area and to eliminate problems associated with yeast and bacteria production.

To clean the nasal fold, gently wipe the fold with a slightly damp washcloth, baby wipe, cotton-tipped applicator, or soft paper toweling. A normal nasal fold may produce a very small amount of moisture and dead hair, usually dark in color, when wiped regularly. Excess moisture, large amounts of black debris, or thick, yellow discharge that has an odor are not normal and should be examined by your veterinarian for appropriate treatment.

Anal Sac Care

Many Pug owners have never heard of anal sacs and are not aware that their Pug even has them until they are hit with a pungent, lingering smell that is unexplained, or their Pug suddenly begins to "scoot" along the carpet.

All dogs have two sacs, one on each side of the rectum, that produce a thin, brown liquid believed to originally have been produced for territorial marking. These sacs are normally expressed during each bowel movement; however, if the fluid is unusually thick or the sac openings are too small or deeply set in, normal expression may be impeded, causing the sacs to fill with fluid. This fluid–filled pocket causes your Pug to feel unusual pressure resulting in his own attempts to express them.

Anal sacs may also express normally when your Pug is extremely relaxed, suddenly startled, or very excited. Some Pugs, however, suddenly begin the scooting routine and despite repeated attempts to relieve the pressure on carpeting and other rough surfaces, fail to relieve the pressure. These Pugs often need to have the sacs expressed manually by a veterinarian or dog groomer. Many Pugs need to have their anal sacs repeatedly expressed or suffer from recurrent anal sac infections and ruptures. These Pugs may find permanent relief by having the anal sacs surgically removed.

Dental Care

The normal canine dentition consists of 42 permanent teeth. Pugs are not normal however, due to their flat facial profile. Flat-nosed breeds suffer from a variety of dental problems. A slightly undershot bite, as seen in the Pug, can be a predisposing factor to poor dental hygiene, tooth decay, and tooth loss.

Pug puppies normally lose their baby teeth around four months of age. During the months that the baby teeth are replaced by the adult teeth, it is not uncommon for those baby teeth, particularly the canine teeth, to remain even after the adult teeth have pushed their way through to the side or inside of the baby teeth. Your veterinarian can remove these stubborn teeth at the time of spaying or neutering, usually around six months of age.

The Pug's short, flattened mouth leads to overcrowding of the adult teeth, which increases the risk for dental plaque, dental decay, and disease. Routine dental prophylaxis, performed by a veterinary clinic, is usually necessary at an earlier age in Pugs than in many other breeds. It is not unusual for routine dental care to begin on Pugs as early as three to four years of age. This process is similar to a human dental cleaning, performed under general anesthesia with an ultrasonic tooth scaler. Don't be surprised if your Pug loses several teeth each time he visits the "doggie dentist." The shape of the Pug's jaw, combined with the crowding of teeth, creates shallow tooth roots. Periodontal disease, which is unfortunately quite common in the Pug, as well as shallow roots equals loose teeth and mouth pain. It is better to remove these teeth under anesthesia than to allow them to remain.

At-home dental care with a Pug can be attempted on a weekly basis using a commercially available "doggie toothpaste and toothbrush," finger toothbrush, or simply a small gauze pad and a baking soda and water paste mixture. Whichever product you choose, the important area to concentrate on brushing is the tooth surface at or near the gum line. Gently massage the teeth near the gum line to loosen plaque and food debris that may be trapped in the gingival pocket, or space between the tooth and the gum. This pocket is the primary location for plaque formation and needs to be attended to regularly to maintain healthy teeth and gums. In spite of the efforts of well-intentioned owners, Pugs tend to dislike having their mouths opened and their teeth brushed.

As a substitute for "hands-on" dental care, you should provide your Pug with toys, chew bones, and food treats that are specifically designed to minimize tartar and plaque formation. Toys and treats that provide friction and abrasive action on the surface of the teeth can be a great addition to your Pug's oral health plan.

Note: If dental disease is a recurrent problem for your Pug, you can discuss with your veterinarian whether a diet change to one of the commercially prepared dental diets may be beneficial. These diets combine a special shape, size, and fiber structure to provide scrubbing action to

the teeth, which decreases plaque and tartar.

Care of the Eyes

The eyes of the Pug are their most expressive, beautiful feature. To keep those "balls of fire" healthy and bright, some attention must be given to them on a regular basis.

The somewhat exposed, prominent globes of the Pug eye seem to be a magnet for dirt, dust, and hair. You should make it a habit to regularly examine your Pug's eyes for any signs of injury or irritation. Should you suspect any problem, do not try to medicate or treat them at home. Eyes are extremely vulnerable to progressive injuries and should be treated only by your veterinarian.

Care of the eyes also involves managing any excess tearing that may occur. If your Pug produces excess tears, carefully wipe away any overproduction with a soft cloth to prevent moisture from building up in the nasal fold area.

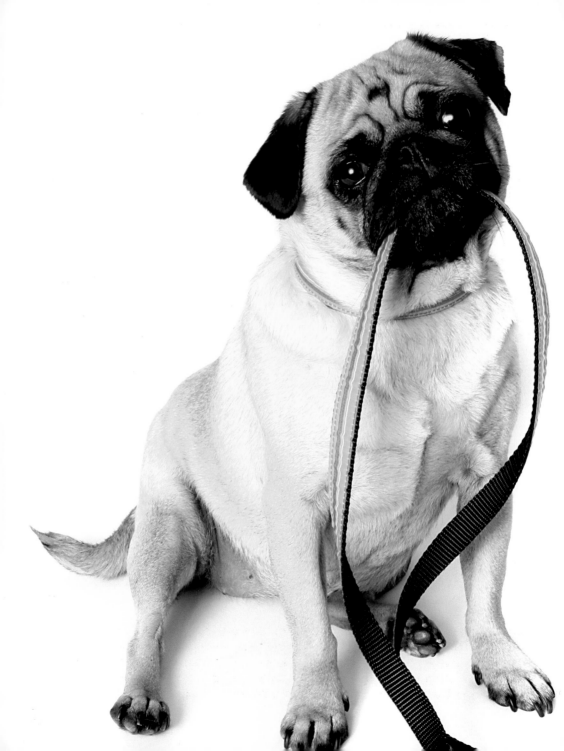

Chapter Eight

Positive Pugs

Pug owners and breeders that have been involved with the breed for any length of time often inform new Pug lovers that there is really no such thing as a "trained" Pug, only Pug-trained owners. The reality is that Pugs generally love to please their owners, exist to be treated as human family members, are extremely intelligent, and quickly learn what they can and cannot get away with. Training a Pug, whether teaching obedience commands, training them for the show ring, teaching tricks, or simply instilling house manners, first involves focusing your Pug's attention on you and then getting through to him what exactly it is that you want him to do.

The Importance of Training

Perhaps the hardest thing for Pug owners to remember and understand is that their Pug really is a dog, not a human, and therefore does not think, communicate, or learn in exactly the same way that a human does. Every task or trick must be broken down into a series of smaller steps that the Pug can easily understand and quickly learn to master. Once the individual steps are learned, they can then be quickly linked together to form a complete exercise.

There are many types of training methods that all claim to be the best, easiest, and quickest for any dog to learn. A large number of books have also been published on dog training, many easy to understand and follow. It is a good idea to read several different books, as no single training method is going to work for every Pug. Combinations of various training ideas and types may be needed to design an effective training plan for your Pug. When the methods described in most training books are broken down, they generally fit into one of two groups—correction-based or force training, or positive reinforcement training.

Correction-Based Training

Correction-based training, also known as force training, is the training method many people became familiar with years ago when obedience training became a mainstay of dog ownership. Modeled after military dog training techniques, correction-based training teaches an exercise by letting the dog know when it has done the exercise incorrectly through a series of corrections, while providing little or no encouragement when the task has been performed correctly. The collar and leash become a tool for the owner to force the dog into a position, as well as providing the owner a method of punishment if the Pug does not comply with the specific task or command.

Correction-based training, although still taught by many obedience instructors, is an outdated form of training. Punishment as a training tool is often misused because owners do not have the proper understanding of how to use it, nor do they have the skill or timing to use it correctly. Many a Pug has been repeatedly jerked at the end of the leash or occasionally choked by a tight collar as the owner tries to teach even the simplest command. The Pug's strong temperament and easily bruised ego often make force training a "battle of the wills," which the Pug owner may very easily lose.

Most Pugs find little pleasure in learning basic, everyday commands using this method. Otherwise happy, eager Pugs often become nervous, sulking Pugs if corrections are all that they ever receive during a training session. Pug owners who choose to train using only force training will be continually frustrated by their Pug's lack of consistent progress and lack of enthusiasm.

Positive Reinforcement Training

Training a Pug by initially rewarding a behavior or task that is performed correctly is known as positive reinforcement training. Training using positive reinforcement is the best way to train a Pug and the fastest way to make a behavior become a habit; it also helps to make learning even the most difficult tasks or activities more of a game than a chore. This approach more easily fits with a Pug's personality, making learning a breeze for a Pug, and teaching a real pleasure for the Pug owner.

Using the positive reinforcement method, the reward is initially given each time the behavior is performed correctly. As the behavior is learned and perfected, the task is performed in a series of repetitions, and the reward is then given on an intermittent basis to randomly reward the correct response. This random reward reinforces the correct behavior and helps to teach the Pug to happily perform the task, anticipating when the reward will be given.

Most Pug owners find that food rewards are the best motivators to use for positive reinforcement training. Food can be used to gently lure a Pug into a specific position, either by smell or sight, and can then be used to quickly reward the Pug when the proper response is given. Toys can also be effectively used to reward your Pug for a job well done.

Clicker Training

Several methods that incorporate secondary reinforcers into the positive reinforcement training method have been introduced, although none have been as successful or as popular as clicker training. Clicker training utilizes a unique, non-emotional sound one, that is not often heard in everyday situations, and pairs it with treats to elicit a prompt, correct response to a specific command or task. Clicker training is really a form of operant conditioning, reinforcing correct behaviors in a positive manner.

Clicker training can be a great tool for training your Pug to perform almost any task. Using the clicker identifies exactly which behavior caused the reinforcement, i.e., food reward, and gives your Pug one more reason to enjoy each training session.

Marker Training

Marker training is exactly the same as clicker training, but a specific word is used to precisely mark when the right behavior occurs. When training a Pug to sit on cue, for example, the word *"Yes"* can be used to mark the instant your Pug's wiggly butt hits the floor. Follow the *"Yes"* with a food reward, given within one to two seconds of the behavior, and you have positive reinforcement training using a marker word!

Basic Training Tools

As with any work in progress, starting with the right tools to get the job done quickly is a key to guaranteeing that the results will be positive. Training a Pug requires the use of several tools, which can be used in combination to produce a happy, willing, obedient companion.

The first tool a Pug owner needs to begin training is patience. Working with Pugs can be a true test of determination—yours and theirs. You must remain calm and focused during the training time, even if your Pug seems disinterested, confused, or defiant. Make it fun! Many an experienced trainer has been perplexed

when trying to train a Pug. The Pug's often stubborn demeanor can challenge even the most seasoned trainer to create a training environment that is fun and interesting, and to produce results that are reliably given on a consistent basis.

Length of Training Sessions

Training sessions should be kept short. As you begin to work with your Pug, only one or two ideas or commands should be taught during any session. The length of the training sessions, as well as the complexity of the tasks that are being taught, can be increased as your Pug learns more basic commands and begins to perform them quickly. Never begin a training session when you are tired or stressed, or the end result will be a Pug that refuses to work with such a grouch! It is also equally important to end each session on a positive note, when the task or command has been completed successfully. Keeping the training positive, fun, and rewarding by controlling your emotions is essential when working with your Pug.

Classes

Just as Kindergarten Puppy Training classes are a great idea for every Pug puppy, enrolling your adult Pug in a beginner obedience class is a wonderful way to begin training your Pug. Participating in an obedience class gives you the advantage of having an instructor who can give you guidance and praise (sound familiar?). Obedience instructors can help you overcome any behavioral problems that you might be having with your Pug, and the added distraction of other dogs in the class teaches your Pug to pay attention to you in situations other than a quiet home environment. Your veterinarian is an excellent source for locating an appropriate class in your area. Local park districts, boarding kennels, and kennel clubs also offer training classes.

Finding the right instructor for you and your Pug is important. Some questions you might ask prior to enrolling are:

• What method of training do you use? Remember that positive reinforcement training works best!

• Am I required to use specific equipment? Many trainers require you to buy special equipment that they are comfortable using.

• How many dogs are in each class? How many instructors or assistants are there in a class? A small class offers a more one-on-one approach, as does a small number of students per instructor.

• May I come and observe a class prior to enrolling? If you are not encouraged to come and watch a class, this might not be a good place for your Pug.

Proper Equipment

When used as an aid in training, the collar and leash become a way for the owner to connect to her Pug, or an extension of the owner's hands, arms, and body. Choosing the right collar and leash for the type of training is critical to the comfort of your Pug, and can help to build confidence or create anxiety if the wrong type is used or the right type is used incorrectly.

Buckle Collars

A simple buckle collar can effectively be used for almost all training sessions involving Pugs, particularly if positive reinforcement training is being done. The buckle collar can be made of leather, nylon, or a combination of both. The properly fitting collar is of sufficient width so as not to pinch or bind on the neck. A buckle collar should not be so loose that it slips off over the head, nor too tight so as to damage the hair. To check the fit, simply place two fingers flat under the collar on the neck and rotate them one quarter turn up. If the collar is binding to your fingers, it may be too tight. If you can slide the collar up over the head with little effort, it is obviously too loose.

Buckle collars are the only choice for puppies enrolled in Kindergarten Puppy Training classes, and an excellent choice for young Pugs in beginner obedience classes. Every Pug, as a means of positive identification, should wear a buckle collar complete with identification tags. It is recommended that a separate buckle collar without tags be used during training sessions.

No-Pull Harnesses

Pugs that pull while on leash are often heard long before they are seen. The constant pressure on his trachea produces a gagging, hacking, noisy approach that sounds as if he is dying a painful death! For these Pugs a harness that allows the leash to be attached in the front, at the chest area, is the right tool! By holding the leash steady in front of your midsection while you stop walking, your Pug is unable to pull. His forward motion will actually cause him to turn toward you with a look of "Huh? How did that happen?" You can then reward him for orienting back to you, which helps to teach him that pulling gets him nowhere, but paying attention to you pays great dividends! A no-pull harness is an excellent tool for every adolescent Pug learning to explore his environment.

Leashes

Choosing a leash is based on what task you are going to teach, or what activity you plan on doing with your Pug. It is not usually necessary to have more than one or two leashes. Leashes generally are available in two lengths: 4-foot and 6-foot lengths (1.2 and 1.8 m). Most training classes recommend and use a 6-foot leash rather than a 4-foot leash.

Leashes are available in several materials—nylon, leather, and chain. Chain leashes are extremely heavy and bulky for a Pug, not to mention the wear and tear on your hands if your Pug tends to pull or jump frequently when walking. Both nylon and leather leashes are lightweight and durable, and offer many style, pattern, and color choices to complement your Pug's wardrobe.

The Wrong Equipment

There are a number of different training tools, which, in most instances, either should not or cannot be used on a Pug. Keep in mind that the Pug is a willing worker when trained in a positive manner, so harsh training or correction methods and equipment that cause discomfort are generally not necessary.

Choke Collars

Choke collars, also referred to as slip collars, may be recommended for adolescent, active Pugs enrolled in basic obedience classes. Choke collars slip over a Pug's head, and tighten when the leash is pulled toward the owner, but should *never* be used to actually choke a dog. Slip collars can be either nylon or a metal chain.

The choke collar is an old training tool whose time has long passed. Unfortunately, many old-school trainers still recommend the use of this tool, insisting that you must correct what you don't want with a strong "pop" of the collar, temporarily cutting off your Pug's airway, or pulling on his neck. Current research has demonstrated that the use of choke collars can lead to tracheal damage, neurological problems such as seizures, and an increased incidence of some eye diseases. For those reasons, the use of choke or slip collars is not recommended for your Pug. There are more positive tools you can use to teach loose leash walking!

Prong Collars

Prong collars are suggested in training situations where the dog needs a stronger correction than the average choke collar can effectively give. These "pinch-type" collars have rows of metal "fingers," which grab the skin and muscle around the neck when the leash is tightened during a correction. These collars do inflict pain, and the added pressure and discomfort often worry a Pug, making the entire training process unpleasant. Owners all too often try to minimize the pinch collars' pressure by using one that is too big, which then renders it useless as a training tool. All in all, the prong col-

lar is not generally needed, or recommended, for training a Pug.

Harnesses

A large number of Pugs are often seen walking their owners. Many of these Pugs share a common accessory—they are all seen wearing a harness. A traditional harness is an excellent alternative to a collar for any Pug that has a medical problem involving the neck, spine, or throat, but should not be substituted for a collar. There is a mistaken belief among Pug owners that the Pug is too sensitive in the neck and throat area to be safely walked with a collar and leash. Think about a sled dog team for a moment. What do those dogs wear to be able to safely pull a heavy sled? Unless it is a no-pull harness your Pug will be able to pull you effortlessly during a walk, while leaving you with no real way to say,

"Hello, remember me back here?" Collars are better tools than traditional harnesses to give you a way to communicate with your Pug.

Head Collar Systems

Head collar systems are a growing trend in behavioral and obedience training. These halter systems offer an excellent way to control a dog during a walk, by utilizing the same pressure points on the head, neck, and muzzle that are used in a horse halter. While these head collars are great tools for use on a dog with a normal head and muzzle structure, the Pug's unique flattened muzzle shape renders them impossible to use on our breed.

Retractable Leashes

Retractable leashes are as common today as halters on Pugs. A retractable leash offers you the convenience of allowing your Pug to feel that he is free roaming, while still being somewhat controlled at a distance from you. Pug owners that do not have a fenced yard find this type of leash a valuable tool for letting their Pug outside, while they are still in the comfort of their home. The Pug loves to stick his nose in places where it doesn't belong, and the danger of retractable leashes is that all too often the Pug is allowed to interact with other dogs at a distance from the owner, and if a fight or problem suddenly occurs, the owner is too far away and cannot react quickly enough to help her Pug. Retractable leashes can also cause burns that are similar to a severe rope burn or other injuries if too much lead is between you and your Pug and you suddenly need to reel in the lead quickly. Common sense should be used whenever your Pug is at the end of a retractable lead.

The Basics

Once you have the right collar and leash, you can then begin to teach your Pug the basic commands that every Pug should know to live a safe and happy life. Training can begin as early in a young Pug's life as you would like. Remember the saying, "You can't teach an old dog new tricks?" Forget it! Even older Pugs can be trained, although they may take a bit longer to want to catch on. Remember, training should be fun and positive, so have lots of small food rewards on hand before you begin your training session.

Teaching Something New

There are a variety of ways that your Pug can learn new behaviors. The most common techniques used to teach new behaviors are luring, shaping, and capturing. Luring is often the fastest way to teach your Pug something new. Luring is simply showing your Pug what you want him to do by having him follow something such as a piece of food, a toy, or your hand. Holding a small piece of chicken above your Pug's head, and slowly moving it back toward his tail, typically makes him lift his head, lower his rear end, and get into a sitting position. Shaping can be a slower way to teach a behavior, but it is more mentally challenging for your Pug. In order to shape a new behavior, you must know the end behavior that you want, and then begin rewarding your Pug for the smallest steps that represent progress toward that goal. Shaping is rewarding small, successive approximations of any behavior. Capturing can be done anytime you see your Pug doing the behavior you want him to learn. You could capture the behavior of lying down by rewarding him anytime he is laying on his favorite pillow or couch.

Watch

Every command should be given when you have your Pug's attention. Before your Pug can begin to learn other things, he must first learn to pay attention to you. This is taught by using a *watch* command.

Beginning with your Pug in front of you and with a food reward in your hand, say your Pug's name. When those gleaming eyes turn your way, put the food reward close enough to your Pug's head so that it is located, give the command, "*Watch*," and bring the food reward up toward the bridge of your nose and between your eyes. Your Pug's eyes should follow that treat up to your eyes, so quickly reward this correct response by giving him the treat. Repeat the process again—name, locate treat, *watch* command, response, and reward. Each correct response to the command *watch* should be quickly

rewarded with a treat. Once your Pug learns to look at you, begin to intermittently reward him with the food treat (every second or third time), or increase the amount of time between the response and the reward (count to five or ten). Your Pug is now ready to learn additional commands.

Sit

The command *sit* is the starting point for many other commands and countless numbers of tricks. When a Pug is in the sitting position, you have the opportunity to teach additional commands, as well as control if a dangerous situation should arise in your Pug's everyday life. Every Pug should be taught to sit, and should periodically be reintroduced to this command.

To begin with the *sit,* it is easiest to begin with your Pug in front of you. Food rewards are used to reward the behavior. Once you have

his undivided attention, place your hand holding the food reward in front of your Pug's nose. Give the command "*Sit*" and move the treat over your Pug's head in a straight line between the eyes and ears. As your Pug's head moves upward to follow the treat, the rear end should balance this action by going down into a sitting position. When your Pug's rear legs begin to bend, give verbal praise by saying, "*Good Pug*" and quickly reward him by giving the treat. Repeat this sequence with each reward being given a bit later as the rear legs bend more and the actual *sit* position is achieved.

If your Pug jumps up for the treat instead of following your hand with his head simply take away the treat, wait a minute, and try again. You can steady the response by placing your opposite hand on the Pug's rear end, just above the tail. Many Pugs try to avoid sitting by backing up and this behavior can be easily corrected. When you begin the exercise, place your Pug in front of a wall so that the rear is not quite touching the wall. There is nowhere to back up at this point, only the option of sitting.

Down

The *down* exercise is a bit harder to learn for many Pugs. Their stubbornness prohibits them from wanting to be in such a position, but once they learn this command, it is often their favorite exercise. *Down* is an excellent exercise to teach for any occasion where your Pug must remain still and in one place for a longer period of time.

To begin teaching the *down* command, have your Pug in the sitting position. Place the treat hand in front of your Pug's nose and give the command, *"Down."* Move the treat toward your Pug's belly, in between the front legs. As your Pug's nose and head move toward the treat, mark the action verbally with a *"Good Pug,"* and reward him with the treat. On each subsequent attempt, your Pug should bend a bit further until the *down* position is achieved, with the elbows and belly on the floor.

The *down* exercise can be very frustrating for a Pug owner to try to teach. Pugs have great staying power when it comes to resisting learning an exercise, and the owner's natural tendency is to become frustrated. There are two hints that may help: one is to work this exercise on carpeting so that the floor isn't quite so cold, and the other is to shape a down behavior, rewarding the bending of the head and elbows in small, progressive increments, rather than only when the *down* position is achieved. Frustration on the owner's part often results in the attempt to accelerate the learning process by trying to push the Pug into the *down* position. A Pug that is a bit dominant will actually resist to a greater degree, and a shy or nervous Pug may be frightened at this physical force. Placing your hand gently on the shoulders, with no hint of real pressure, can steady your Pug if he attempts to back up during the initial downward motion, or once again, you can teach this exercise in front of a wall. The *down* exercise should not involve physical force.

Learning to Come — the Catch Me Game

We have already learned that our Pugs love to have fun, so what better way to teach such an important task than to make returning to the owner a game? The *come* command can be one of the easiest to teach a Pug, the one command that can be a lifesaver, and perhaps the most commonly ignored command because it is incorrectly or incompletely taught.

The command *come* should be taught to every young Pug and should be practiced often. If your Pug ever experiences the freedom of darting out of the front door or slipping his collar, he must respect the *come* command to avoid the dangers of that freedom, namely cars driving in the street. *Come* is the only command that can be used to save your Pug's life when it is responded to immediately.

We approach the *come* command a bit differently than the *sit* and *down* commands. Your Pug should be on the 6-foot (1.8 m) leash and preferably at a distance greater than 4 feet (1.2 m) from you. For puppies this distance can be a bit shorter. Say your Pug's name and when he looks your way, say, *"Come"* or *"Here,"* and quickly move backward and away from him. Your Pug should begin to chase you, at which point you should give a lot of verbal praise. After a few steps, stop and let him catch you. As soon as you have been caught, give a yummy food treat and lots of praise. This should be fun, fun, fun and the more verbal

excitement you can offer during the chase sequence, the faster your Pug will try to catch you. Try to sound excited as you back up, and using a phrase such as, "*That's it*" or "*Good Pug*" in a high-pitched tone of voice will stimulate your Pug to give chase.

If your Pug resists the temptation to chase you, a small, quick tug on the leash toward you as you give the *come* command will start you both in the right direction. If your Pug tends to get close to you, but refuses to actually catch you, try crouching down as he catches you.

As your Pug gets really speedy at catching you, the length of space between you and your Pug can be increased, by using a retractable leash or a long line. To vary this exercise, try shortening the length of the area that you back up and then change direction either to the right or to the left. The key to a quick recall is to use your voice to excite, stimulate, and reward your Pug to quickly return to you, and then use physical praise such as petting or a food reward to reinforce coming all the way to you.

❖ PUG POINT ❖

Rules for a Successful Recall

You need to follow these rules if you want your Pug to come when called:

1. MAKE IT FUN—Your Pug has to want to come when called!

2. MAKE IT REWARDING—Your Pug must believe that coming to you is better than anything else in the universe!

3. MAKE IT TASTY—High-value food rewards are mandatory when teaching this exercise.

4. MAKE IT MANDATORY—Don't call your Pug if you cannot enforce it. If he learns it is optional, he will make the wrong choice.

5. MAKE IT A PRIORITY—Practice this behavior daily for many months in a variety of situations.

Who's Walking Whom

The Pug's small size often causes Pug owners to expect less of him than they would want from other, larger breeds of dogs. Even if you have no intention of ever compet-

Leg Cues

Your legs can become a signal to your Pug as to whether the exercise involves their movement. Starting out with your left leg, as with *heeling,* signals your Pug to move forward. Starting out with your right leg, as with the *stay* or *wait* commands, tells your Pug to remain in place.

things on walks! Think of a dance with a dance partner. You need to teach your Pug partner how to perform the correct steps!

Rule number one for teaching your Pug leash skills is to stop walking when your Pug is pulling! Teach him that walking with you is better by following these steps:

1. Reward calm on-leash behavior. Hold your leash in one hand and fill

ing with your Pug in an obedience trial, your Pug should learn to walk calmly with you.

There are really many different exercises that all come together when you see a Pug walking nicely with his owner. A pleasant, leisurely walk is, in reality, an epic game of follow the leader that may also include a formal "heel" at times.

Loose Lead Walking

Teaching your Pug to walk on a loose lead requires a little bit of patience, some yummy food rewards, and the right mindset. Loose lead walking is different from heeling, which is a much more precise exercise. Don't be too eager to take your Pug for a "walk" unless you have taught him how to walk. To begin teaching your Pug to walk with you, he needs to learn that focusing on you is rewarding; that permission to investigate the world around him comes from you, not pulling; and that self-control is the key to all good

your other hand with yummy, bite-sized treats. Treat your Pug each time he stands still and looks at you. Be patient! Call his name if he is distracted, but resist the temptation to say his name repeatedly. Do not tighten the leash or try to get his attention by tugging on it. Simply wait for him to look at you. Move away from distractions if it seems impossible to get his attention.

2. Once you have his attention, say his name, followed by "*Let's Go,*" and take a step backward, encouraging him to follow you. Treat him as soon as he begins to move in your direction. Praise him for following you, treating every few steps.

3. Change direction, treating your Pug as soon as he changes direction. Keep the initial movement sequences short, five to ten steps at first, treating often.

4. Once your Pug begins to understand that "*Let's Go*" means you are moving together, you can begin to walk forward, treating as often as needed (typically every two to four steps) to keep your Pug's focus on moving with you. Over time you can increase the number of steps between food rewards.

5. Release your Pug from walking with you with the command "*Free!*" That cue means he can sniff, investigate, eliminate, or just relax as long as he doesn't pull you! Move with your Pug as quickly as you need to in order to maintain a loose leash.

The correct *heel* position is along your left side with the Pug's neck in line with your left leg.

Heel Position

Heeling is important for control on walks at times when you do not want your Pug to say hello to others or when you need to keep his eyes focused on you to keep him out of trouble. To remain in this position while walking is somewhat unnatural for your Pug, so the proper *heel* position can take some time to correctly learn and perform.

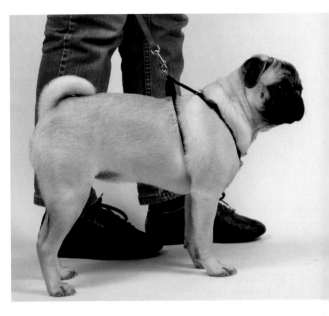

We begin this exercise with the thought of guidance, not physical force or correction. With your Pug sitting on your left side, the handle of the leash is placed in your right hand. Your left hand can be used to hold the leash at a spot closer to your Pug and to hold treats. The leash should be taut, but not tight. Say your Pug's name and then give the command, "*Heel.*" Step forward with your left foot and treat your Pug as soon as he moves forward. Keeping the leash free of slack allows you to maintain your Pug in the *heel* position. Praise your Pug verbally and treat him for remaining close to your left leg. Your Pug now has some idea of where you would like him to be on a walk. If your Pug knows the *watch* command, you can also use this to focus your Pug's attention on you during movement, which hinders the tendency to walk out and away from the *heel* position. A Pug that is in the *heel* position can easily move forward while looking up at you, while one that is too far ahead must stop and turn around to look at you.

Once you have shown your Pug where the *heel* position is, let a little more slack into the leash. If your Pug takes this opportunity to lunge forward, give a short tug backward on the leash and say, "*Get back.*" As your Pug slows and returns to the *heel* position, praise and treat the response. Avoid the tendency to continually jerk your Pug backward as once again this unpleasant aspect to training will negatively affect your Pug's attitude and ultimately his willingness to accept the *heel* position.

Here are two additional tips for teaching and maintaining the *heel* position:

1. If your Pug continuously tries to forge ahead use food rewards during the forward motion given *only* when the Pug is close to your side and in line with your leg. Food treats can also be used to help guide your Pug

Learning to heel correctly takes a significant amount of time, practice, and patience. Once your Pug understands and can correctly identify the *heel* position, try practicing in areas where there are distractions such as a park or busy sidewalk to reinforce this command.

Wait Versus Stay

There are times that a Pug needs to remain still in one place, in spite of his desire to always be at the center of attention. The *stay* command is taught to offer some control over a specific, longer period of time, while the *wait* command is usually a short-term command.

Teaching Pugs to stay can be difficult when their normal instinct is to be moving to wherever the action is. Owners play an important role in how quickly their Pug respects the *stay* command. The *stay* command should be taught in a calm, quiet setting without a lot of distractions, and in a vocal tone that is calm, yet firm. The Pug can mistake any movement from the owner, once the command has been given, for a release signal. So try to remain as still as possible when teaching this command. Your Pug may begin this exercise in any position, though most people choose to start when their Pug is sitting. The *stay* command should always be given in a firm voice, indicating that you are serious about this task.

Begin with your Pug sitting in front of you. When your Pug is in this position, give the command,

in the proper place by luring him and rewarding only when in the proper position.

2. If all else fails, and you have no success in teaching the *heel,* use a repetitive training technique of making a series of quick 180 degree turns. As you are moving forward and your Pug is out in front of you, repeat the command "*Heel*" as you make the about-face turn and continue walking forward. Verbally praise and treat your Pug for also turning and catching up to you, then make another about-face turn while repeating the *heel* command, and walk forward. Again, praise your Pug for catching up to you. Repeat the process. After repeating these turns several times, your Pug should learn that unless he remains near you during the forward walking motion, he might actually wind up behind you and have to play catch-up.

"*Stay.*" Count to three and then give a release command, such as, "*Free,*" and verbally praise him. This is the end of the exercise. Repeat this exercise until your Pug remains still for the entire count.

At this point, you may begin to lengthen the amount of time your Pug remains still. Increase your count slowly to 10, and once 10 is mastered, increase the time to 20, then to 40, and so on. Don't try to increase time, also known as duration, too quickly. Lengthening the stay exercise by two or three seconds each time ensures that your Pug will be successful at this exercise. Work at a successful level for a minimum of three to five repetitions before adding more duration. It is also a good idea to vary the length of the stay exercise so that your Pug doesn't get bored. Sitting still is not their favorite exercise! When the length of time is no longer an issue, you may then begin to introduce the concept of distance during the *stay.* After giving the command "*Stay*" simply take a small step backwards and then pause for a second or two. Return to your Pug by taking a step toward him, pausing for an additional second or two, before you release him. After several successes with one step, you can begin to take additional steps to increase distance. Don't increase the time or distance too quickly, and if any increase results in your Pug being unable to perform the *stay,* go back to the previous length of time or distance. Also be careful not to accidentally pull on the leash as you move or your Pug may take this as a signal to move forward and break the *stay.*

If your Pug repeatedly breaks the *stay,* you may give a sharp verbal correction such as "EGH." The correction must be correctly timed to arrive just as the Pug begins to break the *stay* position, in order to be effective. Learn to watch your Pug's ears and body posture. A Pug that is comfortable with the *stay* will have his weight balanced and will often have his ears pulled back to reflect relaxation. The reality is that if your Pug won't stay, you are probably asking him to stay for a duration that is beyond his level, or at a distance that is too far. Go back to a level you know he can succeed at, and work at that duration or distance.

The *stay* command takes time and patience to learn. Don't expect too much from your Pug as you begin this exercise, especially if he is under one year of age. Young Pugs can often remain motionless only for a period of no more than 30 seconds.

Chapter Nine
The Healthy Pug

Purchasing a Pug from a reputable breeder is the first step in safeguarding your Pug's health. There is no substitute for a healthy puppy, and for those who have had the misfortune of owning a Pug with chronic, long-term health problems, the financial costs and emotional heartbreak are enough to sour their opinion of the breed. Keeping your Pug healthy and happy is your primary responsibility as your Pug's family leader. Choosing the right healthcare team for your Pug is extremely important to your Pug's well-being. You must also be able to make informed decisions that can affect your Pug's long-term health and well-being.

A healthy Pug has a soft, shiny coat, eyes that are full of fire, and an attitude that demands attention. Keeping these traits, which so vividly portray a Pug, is a team effort between you, the owner, and your veterinary team.

Selecting the Right Veterinarian

Choosing a veterinarian for your Pug should be done as carefully as selecting your own doctor. After all, you will have a working relationship with the veterinarian(s) for the next 10 to 12 years, and you will want to be comfortable with the decisions that you may have to make and the quality of care that your Pug will receive.

Brachycephalic breeds (those will flat noses) have unique problems and may need to be treated a bit differently than other dogs. Your veterinarian must be familiar with the Pug's anatomical features and

---

❖ **PUG POINT** ❖

Interviewing a Veterinarian—Questions to Ask

1. Do you refer after-hours' emergencies to an emergency clinic, or is a staff veterinarian on call 24 hours?

2. Do you offer boarding or grooming services?

3. Can I schedule a visit to your practice and receive a tour of the facilities?

4. Do you have a hospital brochure?

5. Are you accredited by or affiliated with the American Animal Hospital Association?

should be comfortable with treating them. Another question that should be asked is whether or not the veterinarian is able to, and willing to, refer challenging cases to a specialist. Veterinarians who are willing to refer patients to other veterinarians with more expertise in a specific field truly have your Pug's best interests at heart. Finally, do not be afraid to ask questions. If you are not comfortable with the level of service or knowledge of the veterinarian or staff, continue to look elsewhere until you find a veterinarian who meets your approval.

The Vaccination Debate

Vaccinations are vital in ensuring that the long-term health status of your Pug remains positive. All puppies receive their initial immunity from their mothers in the form of colostrum while nursing during the critical first few days. This immunity is not long lasting, beginning to wane during the sixth to eighth weeks of a Pug's young life. Vaccinations that protect against the most common diseases are given to prolong, or booster, the immunity that is naturally passed on from the mother.

Risks

While vaccinations most certainly save lives, they are not without some risks. A great debate currently exists over whether pets are routinely overvaccinated, and whether these vaccines may contribute to other diseases, particularly those involving the immune system. Research is currently underway to study the many effects of vaccines, both positive and negative, but for now, the recommendation remains that all puppies receive booster vaccinations during the first six months of life.

Your Pug's diet can affect the immune system's ability to provide an adequate immune response. Antioxidants such as vitamin E, beta carotene, and lutein play an important role in immune response by binding free radicals that can damage fragile immune cells. This damage

Vaccine Titers

The recent debate over vaccinations has given way to new vaccine protocols. Blood tests that measure the level of protective antibodies of a specific disease can be run at a substantial cost by your veterinarian. While titers give you a measurement of the antibodies on that day, there is no way to determine if the protective level will last another day, week, month, year, or longer. Relying on vaccine titers to protect your Pug may be a risky practice.

vomiting, and hyperactivity the most commonly reported. In rare cases, a Pug may suffer from anaphylactic shock shortly after receiving a vaccination. These Pugs become weak, disoriented, experience shortness of breath, and may soon suffer seizures or cardiac arrest if prompt medical intervention is not quickly obtained. You should report any unusual symptoms or activity following any vaccines to your veterinarian as soon as possible. Many veterinarians and breeders do suggest splitting up certain vaccinations to minimize the risk of vaccine reactions.

For those few Pugs that have experienced a life-threatening vaccine reaction, it is usually suggested that additional vaccines not be given.

can lead to a poor immune response and an increased risk for developing disease. Diets that lack adequate amounts of these antioxidants can negatively impact your Pug's immune system response. The Pug puppy's immune system is not believed to be comparable to that of an adult until approximately 16 weeks of age.

Reactions

Pug puppies may experience some minor discomfort, soreness, lethargy, and perhaps even a low fever for a short period of time following each vaccination. Pugs seem to have a higher incidence of minor reactions than other breeds. More severe reactions can be seen frequently in adult Pugs, with symptoms such as facial swelling, hives,

AAHA Canine Vaccination Guidelines

In 2011, the American Animal Hospital Association (AAHA) updated its canine vaccine guidelines in an effort to educate veterinarians and the public with the latest information and recommendations for safely and effectively vaccinating dogs in North America. Since the previous guidelines, published in 2006, new vaccinations have been tested and safely marketed, while some previously administered vaccinations have been withdrawn.

Every Pug should be vaccinated against the diseases that may pose a risk, depending on his individual, unique lifestyle. The decision on which vaccines your Pug needs should be based on his lifestyle risk factors, as determined by you and your veterinarian.

Core Vaccinations

Core vaccines are those vaccines that prevent prevalent, often life-threatening diseases, or those that can prevent diseases that can be potentially transmitted to humans. Core vaccines are initially given to puppies in a series, usually in two- to three-week intervals during the puppy's first two to six months of life. Puppy vaccinations schedules can be extremely confusing, as many breeder recommendations vary considerably from veterinarian recommendations. Thus the Pug owner must decide whose vaccine protocol might be the best for her Pug.

The AAHA recommended core vaccines are:

Distemper

Distemper is a widespread, often fatal disease that occurs most often in puppies that have never received any prior vaccines. Signs of distemper often begin with symptoms that are similar to an upper-respiratory infection. As the disease rapidly progresses, vomiting and diarrhea occur in addition to pneumonia and the possibility of neurological signs such as tremors or "tics."

Puppies should be vaccinated every 3 to 4 weeks between the ages of 6 weeks and 16 weeks, with the final dose being administered after 14 weeks of age, but prior to 16 weeks of age. A single dose should then be administered no later than 12 months after completion of the series. Adult Pugs should receive booster vaccinations every 3 years.

Hepatitis

Infectious canine hepatitis is also known as Adenovirus type 1 and type 2. Hepatitis causes extensive damage to the cells of the liver, as well as a severe upper-respiratory infection. Canine hepatitis is considered to be highly contagious and fatal.

Puppies should be vaccinated for Hepatitis every 3 to 4 weeks between the ages of 6 weeks and 16 weeks, with the final dose being administered after 14 weeks of age, but prior to 16 weeks of age, with a single booster vaccination given no later than 1 year after completion of the series. Adult Pugs should receive booster vaccinations approximately every 3 years.

Parvovirus

Canine parvovirus is a highly contagious intestinal virus that is especially debilitating in young puppies. Canine parvovirus causes intense vomiting and diarrhea and may be accompanied by a high fever. This combination results in severe, often fatal dehydration. The maternal antibodies from colostrum may block the parvovirus vaccine in young puppies for a long period of time, resulting in the need for the final vaccination to be given between 14 and 16 weeks of age. The current vaccinations available today are believed to offer immunity against all recognized strains of parvovirus to date. A single booster vaccination should be given no more than 12 months after the final series booster to ensure that protection from this disease remains.

Canine parvovirus continues to challenge the veterinary community as variant strains have been identified. As new variants emerge, evaluation of the vaccination's efficacy, or ability to offer protection, will continue.

The current AAHA vaccination guidelines recommend that adult Pugs be revaccinated approximately every three years following the initial booster vaccine.

Rabies

Rabies is a fatal virus that attacks the central nervous system in mammals, including humans. It is passed on through direct contact with the saliva of an infected animal, generally from a bite or a scratch. Due to the highly contagious nature of this virus, and the potential for loss of human life, all states require that dogs be vaccinated against this disease. Puppies are vaccinated between three and six months of age, and thereafter boostered either annually or every three years. Contrary to what some believe, there are no two-year vaccinations currently available.

Noncore Vaccines

Noncore vaccines are considered to be elective. They are administered

only if the owner and veterinarian feel that the Pug may be at risk to contract a specific disease.

The AAHA canine vaccination guidelines for noncore vaccines are:

Bordatella

Bordatella is a bacteria that is most commonly thought of as the main cause for canine infectious tracheobronchitis, or kennel cough. Bordatella is highly contagious, but self-resolving in most cases, similar to the common cold in humans. Two routes are currently used to administer Bordatella vaccine: intranasal and subcutaneous injections, also known as parenteral administration. When Bordatella vaccines are administered parenterally to puppies, the first dose should be given at approximately 8 weeks of age, with a second dose administered at 12 weeks of age. Intranasal vaccines offer faster immunity and may be given at a younger age if the risk of contracting the disease is high. Many veterinarians will begin the vaccination series with an intranasal vaccine, which offers protection to puppies attending their first puppy class, and then booster the vaccine with the parenteral injection.

Administration of intranasal vaccinations can be tricky due to the Pug's unique nasal cavity structure and their ability to wiggle away from restraining hands. If too much of the vaccine is lost during administration, a Pug puppy may be left unprotected. Intranasal Bordatella vaccines may also cause a transient cough, gagging, or sneezing in a small number of recipients. This rarely lasts more than a few days.

Annual revaccination is recommended for Pugs that visit day care, dog parks, boarding kennels, or grooming shops.

Parainfluenza

Canine parainfluenza is another part of the canine cough complex, commonly referred to as kennel cough. In adult dogs that are not vaccinated, the symptoms can be mild, but in puppies, the upper-respiratory infection is more severe. Canine parainfluenza in young or debilitated Pugs can lead to pneumonia and can be fatal.

While it is considered a noncore vaccination, many manufacturers include Parainfluenza as part of their core Distemper vaccination. Vaccination recommendations are therefore identical to those of the canine Distemper vaccine.

Borrelia (Lyme Disease)

Lyme disease is a tick-borne bacteria, which produces a low-grade fever, lethargy, loss of appetite, and lameness in some infected dogs. Lyme disease has been reported in many areas of the United States, but not all Pugs are at risk of contracting this disease. Lyme disease can also be effectively treated in its early stages by the use of oral antibiotics.

Should your Pug's lifestyle warrant vaccination against Lyme disease, the vaccine should not be administered before 12 weeks of age. A second dose should be given 2 to 4 weeks after the initial vaccine. Annual revaccination is then recommended if your Pug is at risk.

Leptospirosis

Leptospirosis is a bacterial infection that leads to permanent kidney damage. It is highly contagious and is spread through contact with moist secretions such as urine, saliva, and nasal discharge from an infected animal. Leptospirosis can be contracted from other canine species during woodland walks, from water sources that are contaminated with the bacteria. Few vaccines have caused the controversy that leptospirosis has. It may be one of the primary components that cause severe, often fatal vaccine reactions. The types, or serovars, of leptospirosis that are in vaccines may not protect against all strains of the bacteria. It is a good idea to discuss this vaccine with your veterinarian before it is administered, and to find out how prevalent it is in your area.

Should your veterinarian determine that there is sufficient risk of your Pug contracting Leptospirosis and the decision is made to vaccinate, it is recommended that the initial vaccine be given after your Pug reaches 12 weeks of age. Many breeders recommend delaying the vaccine until after your Pug receives his Rabies vaccination so that the Leptospirosis vaccine can be given separately from any other vaccines. A second vaccination must be given 2 to 4 weeks after the initial vaccine in order to provide immunity. Duration of immunity studies, how long protective antibodies remain, indicate that this vaccination must be boostered annually.

Coronavirus

Coronavirus is a highly contagious intestinal virus that often occurs with canine parvovirus. Symptoms of coronavirus include vomiting and diarrhea. Young puppies are particularly susceptible to this disease, and may require hospitalization and intravenous fluid therapy to prevent dehydration. In malnourished or parasite-laden puppies, this disease can be fatal.

Vaccination against Coronavirus is no longer recommended, as it has not been proven to significantly reduce the incidence or severity of the disease.

Canine Influenza

A new upper respiratory virus emerged in 2004 at a Greyhound track in Florida. The strain was identified as H3N8 and was thought to have mutated from a similar virus found in race horses that also ran on the same track. Outbreaks in other Greyhound racing kennels followed quickly, and by 2006 the disease was confirmed in as many as 22 states and was no longer limited to Greyhound kennels or tracks.

Dogs infected with Canine Influenza have a particularly high risk of developing pneumonia, and as many as an estimated 5 percent of all dogs severely affected with the disease die. Clinical signs of the disease include a moist cough that persists in spite of antibiotics and cough suppressants, a thick nasal discharge, and a low-grade fever. In spite of the severity, many veterinarians do not routinely recommend vaccinating for this disease.

Vaccination against this disease may be considered if your Pug will spend a great deal of time at day care or boarding kennel or attends dog shows. The first dose can be given as early as 6 weeks of age with a second dose given 2 to 4 weeks later. Revaccination against Canine Influenza is then yearly as long as the risk of exposure is present.

Internal Parasites

The prevalence of internal parasites varies from one area to the next, but should never be taken lightly. A Pug that is infected by any one of a number of internal parasites can quickly become unhealthy and may pose a significant health risk to his owner's family and to other pets that reside in the household or visit regularly.

The more common parasites are:

Roundworms

Roundworms are the most common internal parasite, living within the intestinal tract. This parasite is most often transmitted to puppies through the mother's uterus. Roundworms can also be transmitted through contact with the feces of an infected dog or cat. Roundworm transmission to humans is a potential concern, particularly to children.

Hookworms

Hookworms are a nasty parasite, predominately found in warm, humid climates. This parasite attaches to the intestinal wall, and begins to feed on the blood of the poor Pug, resulting in damage to the intestinal lining. This damage decreases nutritional absorption, resulting in black, tarlike diarrhea, and the loss of blood contributes to anemia. Hookworm infection can be a problem in humans as well, as the larval stage of this parasite may be absorbed from infected soil through the soles of the feet.

Whipworms

Whipworms inhabit the large intestines and can result in intermittent diarrhea, weight loss, and a generally unhealthy appearance. Whipworms can be extremely difficult to eradicate completely, as the eggs can lay dormant in soil for long periods of time.

Tapeworms

Tapeworms are one of the few intestinal parasites that do not reproduce within the intestinal tract of the dog. Tapeworms are contracted through ingestion of the egg packets contained within another source such as fleas or the muscle tissue of dead mice and birds. Pugs with tapeworm often have no symptoms, though small ricelike segments may be located in areas where the Pug frequently sleeps. Occasionally, a live segment may be seen near the Pug's rectum.

Heartworm

Heartworms are internal parasites that live within the heart. Heartworms are contracted in the larval stage through the bite of an infected mosquito, with the larvae circulating through the bloodstream and eventually migrating to the heart, where they continue to reproduce. Pugs suffering from heartworms in their early stages often exhibit no symptoms, while those with advanced infections experience shortness of breath, exercise intolerance, coughing, and lethargy, due to the increased number of adult worms present and the resulting damage to the circulatory system. Heartworm disease has been diagnosed in nearly every part of the United States and can be easily prevented.

Protozoan Infections

Two types of intestinal protozoa are commonly diagnosed in the Pug. Coccidia is a small protozoa that causes diarrhea and upper-respiratory-like symptoms in puppies, which seem to be more susceptible to this parasite. Coccidia is prevalent in puppies that are raised in unsanitary conditions. Giardia is a protozoa that causes intermittent or chronic diarrhea. Giardia can be contracted from infected water sources and can be difficult to diagnose.

Treatment of Internal Parasites

Controlling parasites can be easy in some cases, and nearly impossible in others. Roundworms are easily treated with two dewormings, given two to three weeks apart, as the parasite's life cycle is contained within the intestinal tract. Hookworm and whipworm infections can be more difficult to control, as the eggs and larval stages can survive in the environment for long periods of time under optimal conditions. The contagious nature of roundworms, hookworms, and whipworms may result in the need to treat all exposed animals at the same time to avoid reinfection. A single deworming easily cures tapeworm infections, as this parasite does not reproduce within the Pug and is not easily transmitted between housemates.

Deworming agents may be in tablet, powder, liquid or injectable forms. These agents are often very specific in their efficacy toward a specific parasite. If your Pug has been diagnosed with an internal parasite, it is best to have your veterinarian treat the infection with a proven medication, rather than attempt to treat it yourself with over-the-counter medications. Environmental cleanup and control may also need to be part of

---

❖ PUG POINT ❖

Fleas and Tapeworms

Did you know that fleas are the number one source of tapeworm in the dog and cat and can be a source of bubonic plague in humans?

a parasite control plan to avoid reinfection through dirt, feces, and other materials.

Heartworm preventives are currently available that offer protection through oral medications given each month, in the form of a chewable tablet. These tablets have few side effects and may also offer protection against some of the more common internal parasites, strategically deworming your Pug each time the heartworm preventive is given. If you have trouble remembering to give this tablet, an injectable form that time-releases heartworm preventive over a six-month period is also available.

Note: This injection can have some serious side effects and should not be used in Pugs whose health is compromised by other diseases.

External Parasites

External parasites are insects that thrive in the ear canal, on the skin, or live just below the skin surface, causing tissue irritation and itchiness. While external parasites may not cause the severe, rapid health problems that internal parasites can cause, they actually irritate your Pug more and can predispose your Pug to other diseases.

The most common external parasites are:

Fleas

Fleas are insects roughly the size of a pencil point, brown to black in color, and are easily visible scurrying around in areas where hair is limited, such as the belly. Fleas feed on the blood of the Pug, reproduce in the environment (for example, your house), and then die. Eggs are laid in carpeting, hatch into a larval stage, which feeds deep in the carpet on pet dander and other waste material. The egg stage of the flea can lay dormant for years in the environment, waiting for just the right conditions to hatch. The feces of the flea are often seen in the hair coat of the Pug, especially near the tail, and resemble course pepper that has been deposited in the hair coat. This "flea dirt" turns a reddish brown color when rubbed with a damp paper towel, making fleas easy to detect. Fleas cause intense itching in some Pugs, which may lead to self-trauma by biting or scratching. The resulting skin irritation is known as *flea allergy dermatitis*.

Prevention is the key to a flea-free Pug. Many excellent flea preventives are available, most in the form of spot-on products that are applied directly to the skin. If your Pug has already been labeled a "fleabag," eradicating the fleas is a two-part job: Your Pug must be treated to kill the adult fleas that are currently partying on the skin. A flea bath will quickly remove these adults. If bathing your Pug is not possible, oral medications that kill fleas after they bite can be prescribed by your veterinarian. Some oral products continue to eradicate fleas for up to one month, while others are shorter acting and can safely be given daily. Some of these products also inhibit the ability of the

Tick-Borne Diseases

Besides looking really nasty, ticks carry several bacterial diseases such as:
- Lyme disease
- Ehrlichia
- Babesia
- Rocky Mountain spotted fever

flea eggs to hatch, controlling fleas in your Pug's environment. Many of these products also help to prevent internal parasites as well, making them a good choice for preventative medicine.

If you suspect that your Pug has fleas, please contact your veterinarian so that he may recommend the product that best fits your Pug's needs.

Your home must be treated as well, to kill the larval stage and any adults that may be in the environment. A professional exterminator is your best bet for quickly and safely killing fleas in the home environment. All dogs and cats living in the home must be treated at the same time to completely eradicate fleas.

Ticks

Ticks are insects that firmly attach to the skin of the Pug, generally in areas where the coat is sparse such as the ears, legs, and chest area. These areas offer an easy blood supply, which the female tick requires in order to lay eggs. Ticks are found in environments that are cool and damp, and thrive underneath evergreens, in long grassy areas, and in leaf piles. Female ticks are nearly double the size of male ticks, and both sexes increase dramatically in size as they engorge with blood.

Ticks do not cause the overall itchiness that fleas do, and often seem not to bother a Pug at all. They can, however, transmit several bacterial diseases if they are allowed to remain attached and feeding.

To prevent ticks from using your Pug as a "doggie diner," keep away from areas that may be infested such as high grassy areas, bushes, and wooded lots. If your Pug enjoys romps in these areas, check for ticks upon returning home and remove any that you find. A flea and tick spray, lightly applied to the underbelly and legs before visiting potential tick-infested sites can prevent them from ever making it onto your Pug. Spot-on products are also an effective way to control ticks for up to 30 days. Preventive tick collars are less effective and can provoke some irritating skin reactions in Pugs.

Tick removal: Occasionally you might have to remove a tick that has already become attached to your Pug's skin. This is easily accomplished by grabbing the tick with a pair of tweezers as close to the Pug's skin as possible and gently pulling straight out and away from the skin. Do not twist or turn when removing the tick, or you may cause it to tear into two pieces, leaving one still imbedded in your Pug's skin. A spray of flea and tick mist a few minutes before you remove the tick, or a drop of dish soap on the tick itself, may help to loosen the tick and make removal easier.

Never use a match to try and burn off the tick, or apply caustic liquids such as lighter fluid in an attempt to kill the tick. These methods do not work and may cause burns.

Mites

There are four types of mites that frequently affect Pugs. Demodex is perhaps the most common type, affecting puppies and occasionally adults with poor immune systems. Demodex may be localized, affecting a small area usually on the head,

face, legs, or feet, or can progress to a generalized form with a majority of the body experiencing hair loss.

Demodex mites are normally present on the skin, but for reasons usually linked to the immune system, they reproduce in numbers greater than normal, causing hair loss that does not normally seem to itch. The tendency toward Demodex infections is thought to be hereditary in some Pug bloodlines, and animals affected should not be considered for breeding. Demodex is not contagious to other Pugs or animals living within the household.

Sarcoptes infestation is sometimes referred to as mange; in fact, both Demodex and Sarcoptes are considered mange mites. Sarcoptes is highly contagious among housemates and can cause itching for some humans living in the household. Pugs that are suffering from Sarcoptes are often intensely itchy with scaly, crusty hair loss most prevalent on the ear tips, elbows, and hocks. Sarcoptes mites are often hard to diagnose as the female burrows into the skin.

Chyletiella is also known as "puppy mange" or "walking dandruff." Puppies are particularly prone to this mite, and have thick scales on the skin and large flakes of dandruff that may seem to move. This mite spreads from dog to dog through contact and because it lives on the surface of the skin, most insecticides easily kill it.

Otodectes, or ear mites, live in the external ear canal. These mites

Insect Control

Spot-on parasite control products are the newest form of insect control. These products are placed directly on the skin of your Pug and kill external parasites for up to four weeks.

Each product is different, but there are products that kill:
• Fleas (adult and larvae)
• Ticks
• Mosquitoes
• Mites

Spot-on products are considered very safe, but some may cause a local irritation, particularly in light fawn-colored Pugs.

often cause irritation and Pugs with ear mites may exhibit the same symptoms as ear infections, shaking their head or scratching at their ears. Your veterinarian may see ear mites by examining the ear with an otoscope. At home, you might suspect ear mites if the routine cleaning of the ear canal produces a thick, black discharge.

Eradicating mites: Different veterinarians will use a variety of methods to treat mites, depending on the type. Dips may be used to treat for Demodex and Sarcoptes, but may have unpleasant side effects or odors. Ivermectin injections can be safely given to treat all four types of mites, but this use is considered extra-label, meaning the FDA has not

approved it for this use. Some spot-on flea products may kill Sarcoptes and Chyletiella, while ear medications specifically manufactured to treat ear mites may be helpful.

Treating your Pug safely to eradicate mites can be a long and difficult task. Please follow your veterinarian's recommendations to ensure that your Pug is treated safely and effectively.

Anesthesia and Your Pug

Pug owners have heard stories of, or experienced for themselves, the loss of a Pug during or following surgery. The thought of anesthesia can be frightening for a Pug owner, and many choose to put off surgery because of the fear of losing their beloved friend. Understanding how anesthetics are administered can make the reality and necessity of surgical procedures a bit less frightening.

In general, there are two ways to administer general anesthesia—intravenous or inhalation. Both offer the same effect, relaxation and the absence of the perception of pain, however the choice of anesthetic is made for very specific reasons.

Intravenous anesthetics are given through an injection into the bloodstream and are usually given in one dose based on the Pug's weight. Intravenous anesthetics are generally used for short-term procedures. Many have reversal agents that can be given intravenously as well,

to quickly reverse the effects. Most intravenous anesthetics are cleared through the liver and some types may be given prior to the use of a gas anesthetic, in order to allow enough relaxation to place an endotracheal tube.

An endotracheal tube should always be used whenever a Pug undergoes anesthesia. In the event of an emergency, oxygen can then be quickly administered and breathing can be artificially manipulated, if necessary, until normal respiration is restored.

Inhalant anesthesia, or gas anesthesia, is the most frequently used anesthetic procedure in Pugs. The administration of gas anesthesia requires the placement of an endotracheal tube, which supplies the anesthetic directly to the Pug. The dose of anesthesia is based on the desired effect, which can be increased or decreased to produce the appropriate degree of effect, or anesthetic plane. Inhalant anesthesia is generally used for longer procedures, in patients with underlying medical problems, or for cesarean sections. Gas anesthetics are exhaled and not usually processed

through the liver, making them a better choice for many Pug patients.

Risks Associated with Anesthesia

In the best of circumstances, there are always risks associated with anesthetizing a Pug. Complications can be minimized if your veterinarian and hospital staff follow a few simple steps. As a Pug owner, it is up to you to ask questions about your Pug's care throughout the surgical and recovery phases, and to fully understand the risks and complications that may occur.

Pugs can be somewhat difficult to actually administer anesthesia to. Wobbly veins, short, fat legs, and their persistent objection to being held in one spot too long all make intravenous administration a great challenge for even the most experienced veterinarian or veterinary technician. The flat face of the Pug once again creates a problem, since the masks that are used to administer gas anesthesia are not designed to accommodate the lack of muzzle.

During any anesthetic procedure, your Pug's body temperature may decrease, creating a risk of hypothermia. Warming blankets may be used during surgical procedures to keep your Pug's core body temperature from dropping too low. Intravenous fluids, continuously delivered through a catheter placed in one of your Pug's veins, will help keep your Pug's blood pressure stable during the procedure. With a catheter in place, your veterinarian will have a way to immediately administer medications should there be any sudden change in your Pug's condition during surgery.

Proper monitoring during the actual surgery is mandatory to prevent a potentially fatal decrease in cardiac or respiratory function. The veterinary technician or assistant should continually monitor heart rate and respiration rate, and may monitor blood pressure as well. An electrocardiogram, or ECG, may be used to check cardiac function in patients that have a history of heart problems.

Recovery: A large number of the fatalities that occur in Pugs actually occur during the recovery phase of anesthesia, not during the actual surgery itself. An uneventful recovery should take place routinely if two simple procedures are followed during the recovery process: First, the endotracheal tube should be left in a Pug for as long as possible. Anatomical differences, which commonly occur in the Pug, may make the recovery slower and predispose the sedated Pug to a compromised airway; secondly, Pugs should be constantly monitored during recovery until they are able to stand up and maintain proper balance. The period of time between removal of the endotracheal tube and standing, when a Pug is trying to regain full consciousness and balance, is one of the most dangerous phases of anesthesia. If a Pug is not able to

---

❖ PUG POINT ❖

Anesthesia

Isoflurane gas is considered by many to be a safe anesthesia for most long or invasive procedures in the Pug.

Sevoflurane is a pediatric anesthetic that is now widely used in veterinary medicine. Sevoflurane is the best choice for Pugs with cardiac disease, kidney disease, and other internal organ function problems.

maintain balance while lying on his sternum or chest, once again the airway may become compromised, resulting in the Pug falling over on his side and possibly suffocating. The availability of a hospital staff member to keep your Pug upright is a must following any surgery.

Spaying and Neutering

Pet overpopulation is a monumental problem, but one that could be easily decreased with the surgical sterilization of all pets. Altered Pugs are happier and healthier, less moody due to the absence of hormonal changes, and experience fewer behavior challenges related to testosterone and estrogen.

The Spay

Female Pugs that are surgically rendered incapable of producing

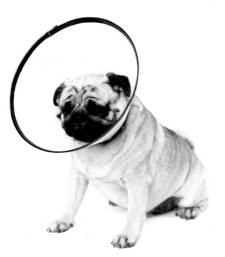

offspring are referred to as being "spayed." The ovariohysterectomy is an abdominal surgery in which the uterus and ovaries are typically removed. Spaying is generally performed before a Pug's first heat cycle, usually between six months and nine months of age. Spaying your female Pug greatly reduces the risk of mammary cancer, completely eliminates the risk of accidental, unwanted pregnancy, and lowers the risk of territorial urine marking in a dominant female.

The Neuter

The surgical removal of the testicles in a male Pug is called castration, or neutering. Neutering is typically performed in Pugs between the ages of six months and one year, before the peak of sexual maturity. The testicles are removed through a small incision just in front of the testicular sac or scrotum, and may be closed with or without sutures. Neutering a male Pug before one year of age significantly reduces the risk of chronic prostate problems, lowers the incidence of malignant rectal tumors, and decreases urine marking. Neutered males are also much less likely to roam in search of female companionship, which reduces the number of unplanned pregnancies. Neutering may also lessen the number of battles of interdog aggression in some cases.

Controversies Surrounding Spays and Neuters

There is a great deal of controversy currently surrounding two aspects of altering dogs—the proper age for the procedure and the "right" technique to use to spay a female dog. Research is ongoing as to the health benefits of surgical alteration versus the health benefits influenced by sex hormones. While removal of the testicles in male Pugs eliminates testicular cancer, and removal of the uterus and ovaries in female Pugs eliminates pyometra and ovarian cancer, doing so before the hormones secreted have influenced potential growth may be linked to an increase in diseases such as hip dysplasia, certain cancers, and immune diseases. There is some evidence to indicate that removal of both the ovaries and uterus may lead to an increase in urinary incontinence. While there is not clear evidence to support a definitive "correct age" or "correct technique" for surgical alteration in dogs at this time, the Society for Theriogenology and the American College of Theriogenologists have issued a position statement, which recommends that the decision on whether to alter be based on each dog's temperament, household, and purpose, through discussion with your veterinarian. Contrary to popular belief, altering your Pug will not change its personality in any negative way. Rambunctious Pugs will still be active, snugglers will still want to be near you, and less active Pugs will still seek their place on the couch. While your Pug's weight may increase slightly following spaying or neutering, obesity has more to do with the natural decrease in metabolism that occurs with adulthood and the owner's failure to decrease caloric intake accordingly, than the actual surgery itself.

Teeth Cleaning

Mature Pugs routinely need to undergo anesthesia and have their teeth cleaned using an ultrasonic scaler. Only under anesthesia can the Pug's mouth be thoroughly examined for loose teeth, fractured teeth, and dental disease. Some Pugs have such severe dental problems that cleanings must be done every six months to prevent excessive gum erosion and ultimately, tooth loss. The mouth is a direct source for bacteria to enter the circulatory system and ignoring dental health can lead to heart problems, kidney and liver disease, and persistent infections.

Anesthesia-free teeth cleaning is available in a very limited number of states, which might sound appealing to the Pug owner fearful of anesthesia. This procedure is not of much benefit, however, as it only removes the tartar visible on the teeth and does not adequately address the gingival margins at the gum line, where plaque and tartar are formed. The procedure can be painful and it is virtually impossible to polish the teeth after cleaning, which increases the possibility of damage to the protective enamel and accelerates plaque formation in the future. Most importantly, a thorough examination of the mouth, including all teeth, is impossible without the use of an anesthetic.

Chapter Ten

Problem-Plagued Pugs

Today's modern canine companions live longer and healthier lives than their counterparts of past generations. No dog, whether purebred or mixed breed, can be guaranteed a life that is free of health problems. Today's Pug is no exception.

Conscientious Pug breeders research health issues and the methods for inheritance of the genetic problems that plague the Pug, and they thoroughly screen all breeding stock for potential health problems prior to breeding. Through careful and informed breeding, great progress has been achieved in lessening the number of health concerns that affect the Pug. Conversely, unscrupulous breeding of individuals can lead to a number of disastrous health issues that often result in long-term discomfort, financial hardship for the owner facing surgical options to correct defects, and altered quality of life of the Pug.

The unique anatomical features of the Pug also make it susceptible to many chronic health problems. Many of these problems are easily managed, while others require more extensive treatment.

Eye Diseases

Perhaps the most common ailments in the Pug are due to the complex nature of the eye and its surrounding anatomy. In many instances, eye problems in the Pug are the result of a combination of more than one specific disease process. A complete and thorough eye exam should be performed at least once yearly by your veterinarian to ensure your Pug's ocular health. Accurate diagnosis of the condition or conditions affecting your Pug, as well as proper and timely treatment, will ensure that your Pug experiences minimal vision loss and discomfort.

Your veterinarian may recommend a visit to a veterinary ophthalmologist, as they specialize in treating many of the common eye diseases that plague the breed.

Keratoconjunctivitis Sicca

Keratoconjunctivitis Sicca, or KCS, is one of the most common eye diseases in Pugs and may be referred to as "Dry Eye." The symptoms of KCS are usually first noted in the adult Pug. KCS results from a

decreased ability to produce the normal tear secretions. The most commonly recognized symptom is a loss of the normal moisture in one or both eyes, and may be accompanied by a brown film covering all or part of the eye. The insides of the eyelids are red and thickened in KCS and may have a constant accumulation of crusty matter. Advanced cases of KCS may lead to eye abrasions.

Due to the thickened and irritated eyelids, your Pug may be misdiagnosed as having an infection or irritation to the eye. Definitive diagnosis is made using the Schirmer Tear Test, wherein a paper strip is placed in the lower eyelid, remaining for one minute with the eyelid closed. Once removed, the moistened portion is measured. A Pug with a 15 + reading is considered to have normal tear production, while 9–15 is considered borderline and should be retested periodically. Any Pug whose tear production is below 9 is considered to have a decreased amount of tears. This lack of tear production leads to KCS.

There are several ways to treat KCS. The goal in treating your Pug is to increase the lubrication of the eye while decreasing any existing inflammation. Most veterinarians prescribe artificial tears placed in the eye several times daily, as well as an antibiotic/steroid drop to reduce inflammation. Care must be taken to verify the absence of abrasions before using any steroids. Two additional medications, cyclosporine and tacrolimus, are widely prescribed to increase tear production when administered on a daily basis. Pugs with borderline tear production may return to normal values within three to four weeks following daily treatment. Treatment of KCS is usually long-term, making this a chronic condition.

Distichiasis

Distichiasis is characterized by a second, abnormal incomplete row of eyelashes. This condition is more prevalent in the lashes of the upper eyelid. Many Pugs with extra lashes exhibit no symptoms, while others may experience chronic irritation, excessive blinking, and abrasions to the eye. Permanent correction is most often done using a process known as cryoablation, or freezing with liquid nitrogen, most often performed by a veterinary ophthalmologist. Surgical excision of the affected lashes can also be a successful treatment performed by your veterinarian. Plucking the lashes is not recommended because the lashes will grow back, changing to a more rigid texture and running the risk of damaging the cornea more quickly.

Trichiasis

Trichiasis is the abnormal placement of normal eyelashes. Pugs are extremely vulnerable to this problem due to the prominent nasal fold and exposed bulging eyes. The result is a constant rubbing of the lashes on the eye and irritation to the cornea, resulting in excessive blinking, corneal abrasions, and pigmentation. The treatment for trichiasis is to return the lashes to a more correct position. In the Pug this requires surgery. Pugs experiencing chronic discomfort must have surgery to decrease the size of the nasal fold or have it removed completely to avoid further damage to the eye.

Entropion

Entropion is simply the rolling in of the eyelid. In the majority of Pugs suffering from entropion, only the lower lids are affected. As with distichiasis and trichiasis, entropion causes excessive blinking and chronic eye irritation, as the lid and lashes rub constantly on the eye. Pugs that experience chronic entropion will have relief with surgical removal of the skin below the eyelid. The resulting scar tissue pulls the eyelid to a more outward position that reduces rubbing and decreases irritation.

Pigmentary Keratopathy

Pigmentary keratopathy, formerly known as pigmentary keratitis, is perhaps the most common eye disease in Pugs. The name of the disease has recently been changed to more correctly reflect that pigmentary keratopathy, or PK, is a specific disease of the cornea and may not be an inflammatory condition, as the nomenclature "keratitis" would suggest. Pigmentary keratopathy is the appearance or increase in a brown pigment, which forms over the normally clear cornea. Pigmentary keratopathy was once believed to have been the result of some other ocular condition, such as distichiasis or entropian. PK can occur in Pugs not suffering from any other eye disease, however, and it is now believed that this disease, may also have an inherited component. Current research into the possible genetic influence in Pugs is ongoing. Unfortunately, the exact cause of the progression of this common Pug eye problem is currently unknown.

PK is easily diagnosed by closely looking at the eye. Presence of a brown, opaque film most commonly occurring in the inner corner of the eye signals pigmentary keratopathy. This opaque film varies from slight to severe. There is no known cure for pigmentary keratopathy, but early diagnosis and treatment can slow down the progression of the disease. In untreated cases, blindness will occur as the film increases to eventually cover the entire eye.

The treatment of PK can be similar to other eye diseases. Any underlying irritating condition should be addressed and treated to reduce the potential for an inflammatory response. Cyclosporine or tacrolimus drops may be prescribed to aid in the delay of further progression of pigment and save your Pug's sight. For any Pug diagnosed with PK the treatment is lifelong. The daily administration of eye drops is necessary, as pigmentary keratopathy will return and worsen if the medication prescribed is discontinued.

Corneal Ulceration

Corneal ulceration is a fancy term for an abrasion to the cornea itself. Once again, the Pug's prominent, bulging eyes make the cornea vulnerable to a variety of injuries, which cause abrasions or scratches. Corneal ulcers are the most common injury in Pugs, and prompt diagnosis and timely treatment is mandatory in preventing further damage or complete loss of the eye.

The most common symptoms of an ulcer are an increase in tearing, excessive blinking, and sensitivity to light. Corneal ulceration is extremely painful as indicated by many Pugs vehemently refusing to open the affected eye. A special fluoroscein stain is applied using a paper strip; it shows your veterinarian the location, size, and depth of the ulcerated area.

The treatment of corneal ulcers or abrasions varies with each individual injury. Scratches to the surface may require no more than an antibiotic drop or ointment applied to the eye several times daily for a week to ten days. Your veterinarian will want to restain the eye after a couple of days to track the healing process. Eyedrops designed to relieve pain may

also be prescribed to help alleviate discomfort for the first few days of healing. The use of oral steroids or eyedrops/ointments containing steroids is not recommended, as these will slow the healing process.

Ulcers that are slow to heal may require a procedure to help speed up the healing process. A topical anesthetic is applied to the eye prior to this procedure. Your veterinarian will then scrape the edges of the abrasion with a cotton-tipped applicator or the blunt side of a scalpel blade to remove dead tissue and allow fresh tissue to begin the healing process. While this procedure may seem excessive, it can be the best way to help your Pug's own body repair the damaged tissue. Home care with antibiotics as described above, as well as follow-up exams should complete the healing process.

Deep or extensive ulcers, or any ulcer that fails to heal with the primary treatment may result in your veterinarian recommending a third eyelid or corneal flap. This surgery provides a natural protective covering to prevent infection, while offering the cornea a chance to heal. The surgical process involves gently pulling the third eyelid of the Pug over the cornea, and securing it above the eye with sutures or buttons. Once in place, the corneal flap is generally left for 14 to 21 days. Your veterinarian will want to recheck your Pug frequently, to ensure proper healing.

Eye ulcers in Pugs can be a medical emergency. Eye ulcers are not only extremely painful for your Pug, but they can result in the rupture of the eye. Seek medical attention immediately if you suspect that your Pug has a corneal ulcer.

Respiratory Problems

The Pug is notorious for its various sounds and idiosyncrasies associated with the flat-nosed breeds. While there are several respiratory problems that can afflict the Pug, the incidence of these diseases is relatively low due to careful breeding. A Pug that is suffering from one or more of these problems is often referred to as having brachycephalic upper airway syndrome. These problems, if occurring in combination, can cause coughing, gagging, exercise intolerance, shortness of breath, and respiratory distress.

Stenotic Nares

When the wings of the nostril are so large that they cover or fill a major portion of the nasal openings, the Pug in question is suffering from stenotic nares. The resulting loss of air passage causes excessive snorting or snoring, coughing, and gagging. An examination of the nostrils confirms the diagnosis. Any Pug with stenotic nares that hinder normal breathing must have surgery to open up the affected nostril. This procedure is often recommended in young Pugs.

Elongated Soft Palate

Pugs suffering from the symptoms associated with brachycephalic upper airway syndrome may be diagnosed with an elongated soft palate. The normal soft palate barely overlaps the airway passage. In many Pugs, the soft palate is too long, thereby reducing the normal airway passage. These Pugs often cough, are "noisy breathers" especially during hot weather or exercise, and in severe cases have extreme difficulty in breathing. Visual examination and therefore, diagnosis, can be tough in a Pug, and the only effective treatment option is surgical shortening of the palate.

Collapsing Trachea

Tracheal collapse is a reduction in the diameter of the airway due to the weakening of the cartilage, which forms and supports the trachea. Collapsing trachea is a disease commonly affecting the middle-aged to older Pug, and is often first noticed as a dry, honking cough. In Pugs suffering from tracheal collapse, the cough is often worsened during exercise, excitement, heat, and humidity,

as the normal airway is reduced in diameter or pinched. Obese Pugs are at a significantly higher risk and many suffer from such severe collapse that their inability to breathe normally is frequently noticeable.

X-rays of the airway can diagnose the majority of Pugs afflicted with tracheal collapse as they breathe in and out.

The treatment of a Pug with tracheal collapse in most cases is aimed at reducing the severity of the episodes of coughing. Mild sedation or cough suppressants are often prescribed for otherwise healthy Pugs. Nutritional supplements to strengthen cartilage may also be beneficial.

While there are surgical options to treat this disease, they are difficult to perform and not without risk. Artificial rings can be surgically placed to help hold the trachea open, or a stent can be inserted to help improve rigidity of the trachea. These procedures are typically performed by only veterinary surgical specialists and may not be well tolerated by all Pugs. They can also be cost prohibitive for many Pug owners, making medical management of this disease a more practical choice.

Reverse Sneeze Syndrome

While not generally thought of as a disease process, reverse sneeze is thought to be the result of excessive postnasal drip in the Pug. Reverse sneeze may be linked to allergies, though this has not yet been proven. There are very few Pugs that do not experience this syndrome at some point, and while the sound may be very frightening for a Pug's owner, reverse sneeze syndrome is non-life threatening and can disappear as quickly as it comes.

A Pug experiencing reverse sneeze may initially look and sound as though he is choking, extending the neck and sometimes arching his back. While in a normal sneeze there is the exhale of air, with a reverse sneeze the Pug is inhaling and accompanying this inhalation is a short, snorting noise that mimics or sounds like a deep cough or loud snore. Reverse sneeze episodes last from a few seconds to a minute or more and may spontaneously reoccur.

There is no treatment necessary for reverse sneeze syndrome. Pugs that have been diagnosed with allergies may benefit from an antihistamine to lessen postnasal drip. Many owners have found that placing their thumb over the nostrils, temporarily reducing the influx of air, reduces the severity and duration of the episode.

Lung Lobe Torsion

A rare but life-threatening condition that seems to affect Pugs more often than other small breed dogs is a condition where one or more lobes of the lung spontaneously turn or twist, causing obstruction of the trachea, lymphatic vessels, and blood vessels. Typically thought of as a disease of large, deep-chested dogs, the underlying cause of this disease in Pugs is currently unknown. Pugs suffering from lung lobe torsion are often acutely short of breath, may seem weak, may attempt to cough or wretch, and ultimately go into shock due to a compromised circulatory system. Your veterinarian may diagnose this disease after taking X-rays of your Pug's chest. Lung lobe torsion is a medical emergency, as surgical intervention to remove the involved lobe is the only treatment. Quick diagnosis and treatment is necessary to minimize damage to the surrounding vessels.

Orthopedic Concerns

Perhaps the most debilitating diseases currently facing the Pug are orthopedic in nature. While efforts to eradicate these diseases have been on the rise in recent years, Pug breeders still have a long way to go before these problems have been completely eliminated.

Patellar Luxation

The normal Pug stifle or knee is a complex joint, containing the patella or kneecap. The stifle connects the femur or thighbone to the tibia and fibula located in the lower portion of the leg. Proper alignment and func-

tion of the knee is crucial to proper mobility.

Patellar luxation is thought of as the most common orthopedic ailment affecting the Pug today. This defect is not usually present at birth, as the changes affecting patellar luxation often occur during the growth of a young Pug up to one year of age. Patellar luxation is generally considered a hereditary defect, and affected Pugs should be eliminated from breeding programs. Patellar luxation in the Pug can occur in one leg or both legs.

The normal patella sits deeply positioned in a groove and is secured by the quadriceps tendon. With normal motion, the patella slides up and down with each flexion or contraction of the quadriceps muscle. When the groove is too shallow to accommodate the patella, or the tendon is unable to stabilize the joint during movement, the patella moves inward, causing the knee to luxate or "pop"

❖ PUG POINT ❖

OFA

The Orthopedic Foundation for Animals (OFA) is the most commonly recognized organization for hip conformation evaluation. The most recent OFA statistics indicate that Pugs rank second of the breeds most affected with hip dysplasia. Currently, 60.8 percent of the Pug radiographs submitted to OFA are affected with hip dysplasia to some degree.

out of place during movement. Patellar luxation can also occur laterally (outward), though medial luxation is more common in the Pug.

A grading system is generally used to indicate the severity of the luxation:

Grade 1: Luxation is considered intermittent, and the affected limb is carried occasionally during movement. The limb position returns to normal after a few steps.

Grade 2: Luxation is considered frequent, with the affected limb held up the majority of the time during forward movement. The patella can be easily moved out of place. While many Pugs live with this condition, bony changes occur over time, causing rubbing or grinding and eventual arthritic conditions.

Grade 3 and Grade 4: In Grade 3 luxation, the patella is permanently displaced; however, the Pug is able to occasionally put weight on the affected leg. With Grade 4 luxation, the permanent displacement renders the limb incapable of bearing any weight. Grade 3 and Grade 4 luxation require surgical correction to restore normal mobility and eliminate pain. Early surgery will minimize the arthritic changes and decrease the need for medication to control pain.

Legg-Perthes Disease

Legg-Perthes disease is a painful debilitating condition characterized by a breakdown of the top of the femur or thighbone. This disease is genetic in nature and, as with patellar luxation, affected animals should not be bred.

Legg-Perthes is most commonly thought of as a disease affecting only one leg, though cases of bilateral Legg-Perthes are reported. The normal age of onset is 5 to 8 months of age, but Legg-Perthes has been reported in Pugs from 3 months of age to 13 months of age.

The Pug affected with Legg-Perthes will exhibit sudden to chronic lameness, chewing at the hip or flank area (an indication of pain), and an abnormal gait. Reluctance to go up and down stairs may also be seen. Diagnosis is made by radiographic evaluation of the hip joint.

The treatment for Legg-Perthes is surgical excision or removal of the head and neck of the affected limb. This corrective surgery produces excellent results, and recovery time is minimal. Once recovered, a slightly abnormal gait may remain due to the difference in length of the hind limbs.

Hip Dysplasia

Hip dysplasia is perhaps the most underreported and underdiagnosed orthopedic condition that affects Pugs. Hip dysplasia is a complex disorder thought to have a moderate inherited component. It is defined as any structural abnormality that affects the proper fit of the head of the femur bone into the pelvic hip socket. The diagnosis of hip dysplasia is made through X-rays of the hip joint and is classified based on one or more of nine recognized anatomical deviations from normal hip conformation. The Pug ranks second in the incidence of hip dysplasia among all breeds, with an astounding 67.1 percent of all Pugs recorded as dysplastic by the Orthopedic Foundation for Animals.

A Pug with mild hip dysplasia may have no symptoms, while severely affected Pugs may experience hip/joint pain, lameness, and degenerative joint disease. Foreleg lameness may also be present as the Pug attempts to shift a disproportionate amount of weight from the hind limbs to the forelegs.

Once a diagnosis of hip dysplasia has been made, treatment options must be discussed based on the age of the Pug and the severity of the disease. If diagnosis is made early, a triple pelvic osteotomy (TPO) may be performed in which the hip is rotated and several metal pins and plates are used to stabilize the femoral head. This stabilization creates a more functional position for the pelvis. In adult Pugs, complete removal of the affected head and neck of the femur may be performed or a total hip replacement may be suggested as an option. Any arthritic changes should be managed with anti-inflammatory medications and amino acids to increase joint fluids. These amino acids ease pain naturally and lubricate the joints for better range of motion.

Hemivertibrae

Hemivertibrae is a malformation that occurs before birth and is characterized by a failure of fusion between the left and right sides of one or more vertebrae. This malformation causes a shortening or misshape of the vertebrae. If more than one vertebra in a row is affected, or a single vertebra is too small to accommodate the spinal cord, the Pug may experience numbness and potential paralysis. Hemivertibrae often results in a curvature of the spine. The onset of hemivertibrae is usually detectable at six to eight months of age, though most cases go undetected or are discovered on X-rays for other medical problems. Hemivertibrae occurring at the base of the neck results in rear leg numbness or lameness, and loss of control of the rear limbs. There is no universally accepted treatment of hemivertibrae. In young Pugs afflicted with hemivertibrae and suffering from spinal cord compression, surgery to reduce the pressure on the spinal cord may be useful in regaining mobility.

Constrictive Myelopathy

An emerging neurological disease that seems to be present in middle-aged Pugs at an alarming rate is constrictive myelopathy, or CM. This disease affects the rear legs of Pugs and may be difficult to correctly diagnose without advanced imaging such as CT scans or MRI, as the same neurologic deficits can be seen in Pugs with intervertebral disc disease or spinal trauma. Pugs with CM have a progressive loss of muscle coordination in the rear legs and often drag their feet when walking. Urinary and fecal incontinence are common complaints from owners prior to loss of normal rear leg function. CM is progressive and will result in the eventual paralysis of the rear legs. Pugs suffering from CM are not in pain and seem to enjoy their day-to-day activities as if nothing is wrong.

The initial research into CM indicates that most, if not all, Pugs are born with abnormally small joints between vertebrae. The defective development of these joints may be a breed anomaly, and research seems to indicate that Pugs that develop constrictive myelopathy have fibrous tissue development around a specific section of the spinal cord, which may be caused by the instability of the spinal column. It is unknown whether there is a genetic component to the formation of this tissue at this time.

There is no truly effective treatment currently available for Pugs suffering with CM. Surgical cord decompression and stabilization of the affected area of the spinal column may slow the disease progression, but may not return function to the rear legs or improve incontinence issues. Pugs

that develop symptoms of rear limb ataxia should be seen by a veterinary neurologist or surgeon at the time of onset. A Pug affected with CM can require significant home nursing care due to the inability to control both urine and stool. The debilitating effects of this disease often force owners to make a difficult decision to euthanize their beloved Pug well before he reaches normal life expectancy of 12 to 14 years.

Ear Problems

Conditions affecting the ear in Pugs are mainly due to a lack of routine cleaning of the ear canal. Regular cleaning is essential.

Otitis Externa

Inflammation of the ear is often described as otitis externa. Otitis externa refers to inflammation or infection in either one or both of the vertical and horizontal ear canals. Otitis may appear suddenly or be a chronic problem with the canal appearing to be wet, red, swollen and sometimes bleeding. Brown, black, or puslike discharge is usually present and may have a strong, objectionable odor.

The exact causes of otitis externa include excessive wax production, excessive moisture, allergies, bacterial and fungal infections, yeast, and parasites. The Pug suffering from even a mild case of otitis externa may exhibit signs of pain—shaking of the head, rubbing the affected

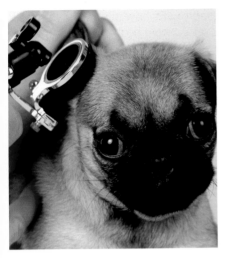

Dermatological Problems

Skin diseases are the most frustrating problems that a Pug owner can encounter. Many of these diseases are difficult to diagnose, tough to treat, and impossible to cure. Unscrupulous breeding often results in a poor immune system, which can contribute to some dermatological problems.

Pyoderma

Pyoderma is a bacterial skin disease most commonly caused by staphylococcus or streptococcus. Small red bumps are usually present, with reddened skin occurring in affected areas. Dry, crusty areas and possible hair loss also accompany pyoderma. Pyoderma can occur anywhere in the Pug, but the most commonly affected areas are the facial folds, lips, and between the toes.

By clipping the affected area and cleansing with antiseptic soap, pyoderma is usually controllable. Routine cleansing of the area, as well as oral or topical antibiotic therapy may be needed.

Acne

Pyoderma on and around the chin area is common in young, adult pugs. These pimples are referred to as acne and are small to moderate in size. Generally, no treatment is required to control acne; however, the use of over-the-counter acne cleansing pads may speed healing and prevent further pustules from

side of the face on objects, and pawing at the ear.

To determine if your Pug is suffering from otitis externa, your veterinarian will examine the ear canal with an otoscope. Microscopic evaluation of any discharge for the presence of fungus, yeast, or mites may be suggested, as well as a culture and sensitivity test to determine the exact bacteria present and which antibiotics will be most effective in treating the infection. If ear mites are present, this condition must be treated as well and all animals in the household may need treatment at the same time to eradicate the mite.

Chronic otitis externa can be extremely difficult to completely cure and is frustrating for the Pug, the owner, and the veterinarian alike. If all diagnostic tools have been utilized and all treatment options have failed, surgery to permanently open the ear canal may be needed to offer relief.

developing. When using these pads, extreme care should be taken not to get any medication in or near the eyes.

Allergic Dermatitis

Allergic dermatitis is classified as hypersensitivity to any allergy-causing substances, known as allergens or antigens. Also referred to as atopic dermatitis, allergies in Pugs most often manifest themselves in the skin, with the feet, chest, ears, abdomen, and anal areas most commonly affected.

The allergic Pug is extremely itchy. The skin is deep pink to red in color, and constant scratching or licking leads to self-mutilation and thus, in turn, the potential for bacterial infection. Often, with atopic dermatitis, there is hair loss in the areas where bacterial sores are present.

The causes of allergic dermatitis are extremely numerous and differ with each Pug. Some of the more common causes include

Flea allergy dermatitis: An oversensitivity to the saliva of the flea.

Pugs with flea allergies will chew their tail head and may jump suddenly to chew when a bite occurs. Severely sensitive Pugs will react to one or two fleas, while others can tolerate hundreds with little or no discomfort.

Inhalant allergy: Allergies to molds, pollens, and plant spores may often be referred to as seasonal allergies. These Pugs are itchy each year at the same time, and changes in the weather often bring much-needed relief.

Food allergy: Food allergy is the body's reaction to a normal protein or carbohydrate source in the Pug's diet. Pugs with true food allergy usually have red earflaps, face, feet, chest, and abdomen. Your veterinarian may recommend feeding a diet with a unique protein and carbohydrate source or a hydrolyzed protein diet to diagnose food allergy. Hydrolyzed protein diets include foods that have their protein source broken down into tiny molecules, which the body is unable to recognize as an allergen. These diets are gaining in popularity, but the lengthy process to produce the diets increases their cost significantly.

In treating the allergic Pug, remember that most allergies are controlled, not cured. Diagnosis of the true, underlying hypersensitivity needs to be determined. Accurate diagnosis often requires elimination over a period of time. If the hypersensitivity can be determined, as in flea allergy dermatitis, elimination of the source of the antigen is necessary to cure the allergy. Antibiotic therapy is indicated for any secondary bacterial infection and may need to be continued long-term. Corticosteroids may be used to relieve intense itching.

Allergy testing can be done in the Pug with injections of specific antigens created to desensitize him. Many owners report excellent results, while others indicate that their Pug received little or no relief.

Seizures and Pug Dog Encephalitis

Seizure activity is a frequently reported problem in the Pug. This affliction is frightening for the unsuspecting Pug owner to witness, and often causes the Pug moderate confusion following seizures.

Pug Dog Encephalitis

Pug dog encephalitis, or PDE, is also known as necrotizing meningoencephalitis, or NME. NME is an inflammatory disease of the central nervous system, once thought of as specific and unique to the Pug. Through ongoing research, we now know that NME can occur in other small breeds. Although less than 2 percent of all Pugs will succumb to this disease, its devastating effects on the owner and breeder make it a dreaded diagnosis. PDE is characterized by inflammation of both the brain and the outer membranes and can be definitively diagnosed only once death has occurred. Although NME has been reported for some time in Pugs, there are many questions still unanswered.

PDE generally affects young Pugs, with fawn, female Pugs under the age of 7 seemingly more likely to develop the disease than males or black Pugs. Early symptoms include reluctance to go down stairs, circling, weakness on one side of the body, and blindness, with these symptoms rapidly progressing to seizure activity. Seizures in the Pug afflicted with Pug dog encephalitis may first respond to conventional anticonvulsant therapy with diazepam and phenobarbital; however, recurrent, multiple seizures that fail to diminish with treatment soon follow.

Pug dog encephalitis has a rapid rate of progression. Coma, followed by death, occurs within two weeks of the onset of seizure activity. There are no known survivors of Pug dog encephalitis to date and no known cure.

Pug dog encephalitis research has been ongoing, thanks to the support of many Pug breeders and owners who have submitted blood and tissue samples, and the veterinarians who have so tirelessly pursued research on the disease. PDE is particularly devastating to owners who are ill-prepared for the sudden loss, as well as to breeders who face a potentially lethal defect in their breeding program.

Through collaborative research efforts, a genetic marker test focusing on a specific region of dog chromosome 12 is now available through the

University of California-Davis Veterinary Genetics Laboratory (VGL). While this test does not diagnose the disease itself, it is another tool that breeders can use to make informed decisions when considering breeding their Pug.

A cheek swab sample sent into VGL will reveal one of the following results:

N/N—These Pugs are homozygous normal, with a low risk for developing NME

N/S—These Pugs are heterozygous normal, with a low risk for developing NME

S/S—These dogs have two copies of the NME marker and are 12.75 times more likely to develop NME

The most current research also indicates that a second region of dog chromosome 8 may also influence which Pugs ultimately develop NME. Further research is needed not only to identify all of the factors that influence the development of the disease, but also to ultimately find a way to prevent it from occurring. For now, genetic testing and selective breeding is the Pug's best bet!

Idiopathic Epilepsy

Epilepsy, which has no determined cause, can occur in the Pug at any age. Diagnostic blood work should be performed to rule out an organ dysfunction as the cause, as well as a fecal sample to rule out internal parasites.

Conventional anticonvulsant therapy is usually effective in controlling the seizures. Epileptic Pugs on medical therapy should have yearly blood

levels checked to ensure that the medications are at the proper levels, as well as blood chemistry screenings to monitor organ function. Pugs with controlled idiopathic epilepsy usually lead normal, healthy lives.

Mast Cell Tumors

Mast cell tumors are one of the most prevalent tumors in Pugs. Mast cells originate from bone marrow and contain histamine, which is released during allergic reactions or trauma to the skin. Mast cell tumors are considered malignant, though some are not as likely to recur or spread to other areas of the body.

Mast cell tumors may look like a variety of other common non-malignant tumors, so a proper diagnosis is important. A fine needle aspirate and subsequent staining of the content reveals a very distinct cell type. Complete surgical excision of the tumor, with wide margins of the affected area, and a biopsy will reveal the "grade" of tumor, typically 1, 2, or 3. The grade may help determine the likelihood of